Carving Characters

with Jim Maxwell

FOX CHAPEL
Fox Chapel Publishing
Box 7948
Lancaster, Pennsylvania 17604

Library of Congress card # 82-90147

"Carving Characters with Jim Maxwell" is a slightly altered reprint edition of "Carving Caricatures from the Missouri Foothills" originally published by the author.

Interior photograph by Don Kaiser, Kaiser Studios, Clinton Missouri.
Cover photography by Bob Pollet, VMI Productions, Leola Pennsylvania.
Cover design and typography by Brian S. Reese.

Manufactured in the United States of America
93 94 95 96 1 2 3 4 5 6

You may order additional copies of this book for the cover price plus $2.50 shipping. Try your bookstore first!

Fox Chapel Publishing
Book Orders
Box 7948
Lancaster, PA 17604

FOREWORD

It is hardly surprising that the hectic pace of modern life has inspired a back-to-basics movement that includes an appreciation for handcrafting items in natural forms. In ever-increasing numbers, people are turning to the creative arts as a means of tuning out their frustrations and tuning in to themselves.

Whittling was once considered simply a pastime for old men on front porches. Woodcarving satisfies the creative and leisure need of people of all ages, occupations, and levels of ability so well. Whittling and woodcarving is now properly recognized as an art form and has also become one of the fastest-growing hobbies in America.

Woodcarving can be an inherited or an acquired art. There are those who seem to have been born with both the desire and the ability to created in wood. But most carvers developed their interest quite by accident: through attending an art fair with a friend; picking up a book on the subject; or perhaps meeting and talking with an interesting woodcarver.

Once their interest is kindled, some carvers exhibit a natural skill and are quickly whittling their own creations. Others enjoy working from a book with step-by-step instructions explained by an advanced or master woodcarver who is willing to share his patterns and techniques.

Jim Maxwell is such a woodcarver. Born and raised in the Missouri foothills, near the lake of the Ozarks and Truman Dam area, he developed a natural love for wood and woodcarving while working at his father's sawmill. Through this book, he shares his knowledge and experience while providing patterns and explaining the techniques and procedures used in carving twelve humorous figures.

But this is more than a book of woodcarving patterns. It is a narrative in native art of a region's history. One wonders about Jim's patterns. Are they caricatures of people he has known? Or are they creations of his imagination, real only in their historical perspective? Only Jim Maxwell knows for sure. But whichever they are, they are designed to be carved and enjoyed by all.

CONTENTS

SELECTING WOOD AND TOOLS

TOOLS

Because this book deals primarily with patterns and ideas for the intermediate or student carver, I will not spend a great deal of time on the simple step-by-step methods of whittling and tool sharpening. Most carvers who are looking for new ideas and patterns have already obtained a knowledge of tool sharpening and basic whittling. If not, there are several good books for beginners on the market.

The tools I use for making the projects in this book are the same as those found in most basic or beginner sets:

- A small, thin-bladed knife
- 3mm v-tool
- 6mm v-tool
- 2mm deep gouge
- 4mm deep gouge
- 6mm deep gouge
- 12mm shallow gouge

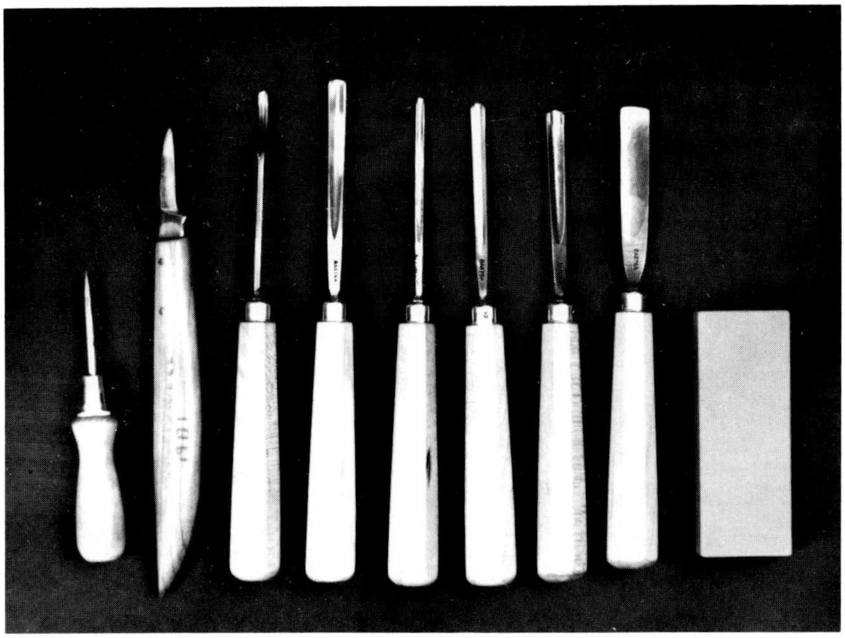

Figure 4 — Basic carving tools and sharpening stone. With these basic tools and the ability to keep them sharp, you should be able to carve any project in this book.

WOOD

Basswood, or linden wood, was used for every project in this book as it is my favorite. However, there are several other woods that can be used with good results. I have also used sugar pine, catalpa, sassafras, and white pine on many other projects.

LINDEN WOOD

Linden: any of a genus of trees (family: TILIA, the linden family) having large oval or heart-shaped leaves with toothed edges and cymose yellowish flowers rich in nectar. A. A European tree used for ornamental planting. B. A tall North American forest tree, also called Basswood.

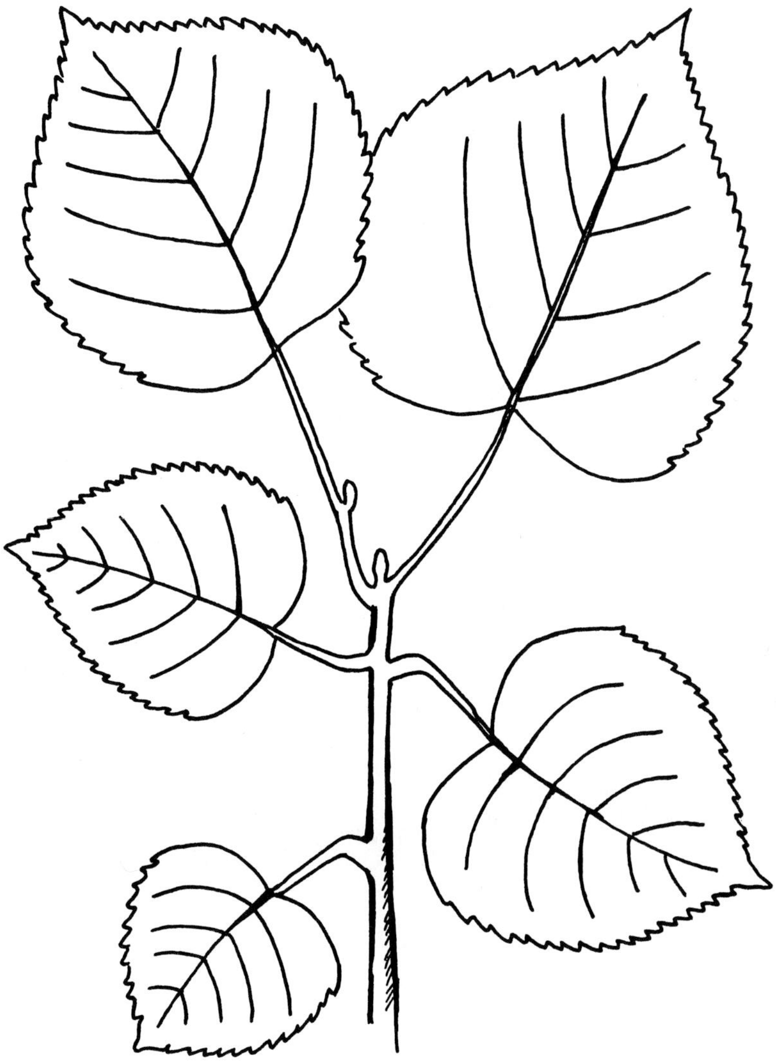

Figure 5 — Linden or basswood leaf

We will begin by carving some of the easier projects first, with step-by-step instructions and photos. As you become familiar with the methods and techniques I use in carving caricatures, it will not be necessary to repeat the same basic instructions over and over for each figure. Our attention will focus, instead, on ideas so that you, as a fellow carver, may become more aware of the possibilities around you for creating new and original caricatures of your own.

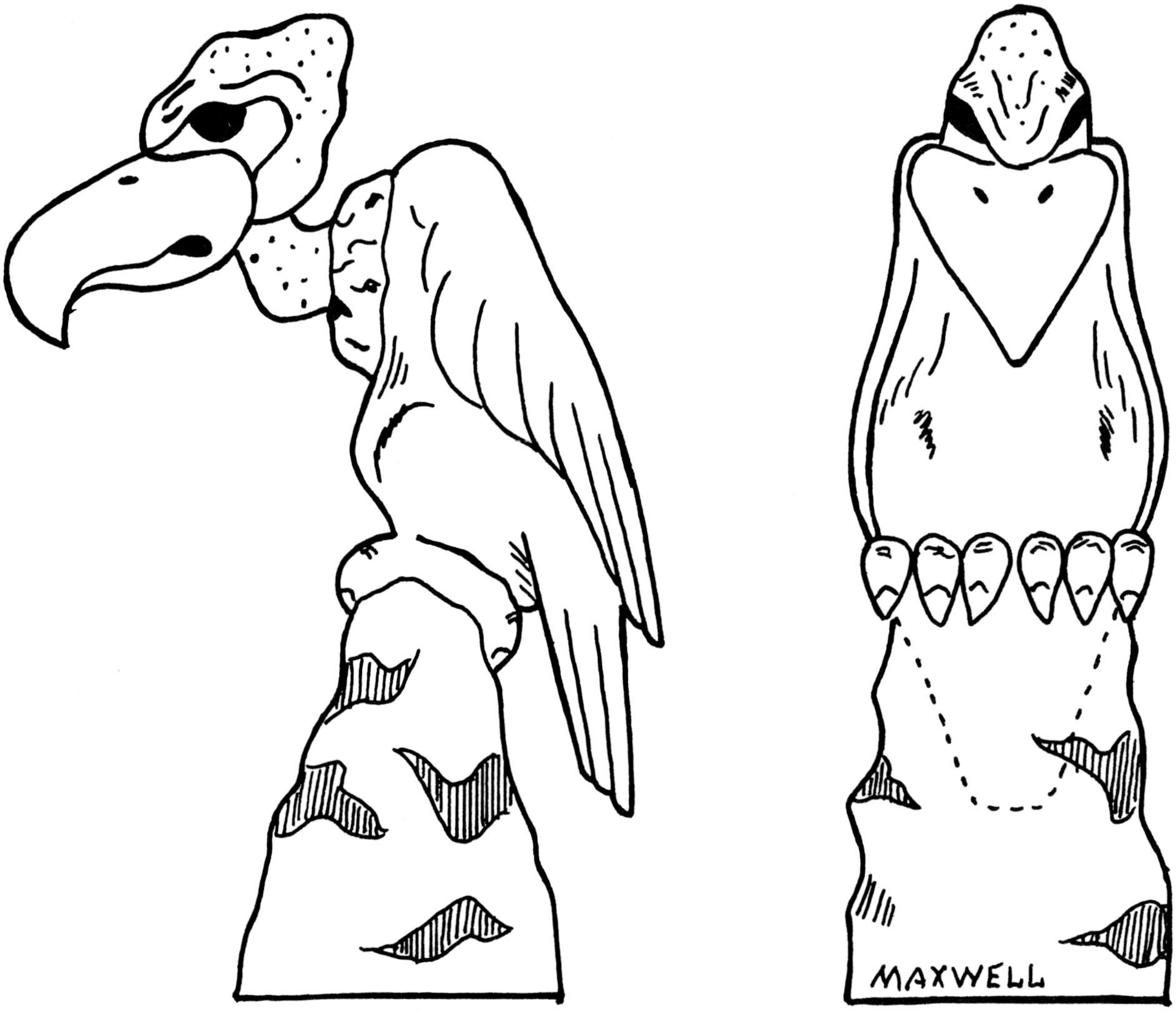

Figure 6 — Pattern for the Buzzard

THE BUZZARD

Soaring high above the limestone bluffs along the Osage river in Springtime, big black buzzards court their mates and prepare their nests in the rocky crevices below. Such vultures abound in the foothills of Missouri. To me, they were simply big, black, ugly birds. Then, in 1963, I noticed an old buzzard in the "Tumbleweeds" comic strip. If a cartoonist can make such an interesting caricature out of an ugly old bird, I thought, why not whittle a 3-dimensional buzzard from wood? My first buzzard got lots of laughs. Before long, I was putting buzzards on mountaineer clocks, piles of bleached bones, and other humorous caricature scenes.

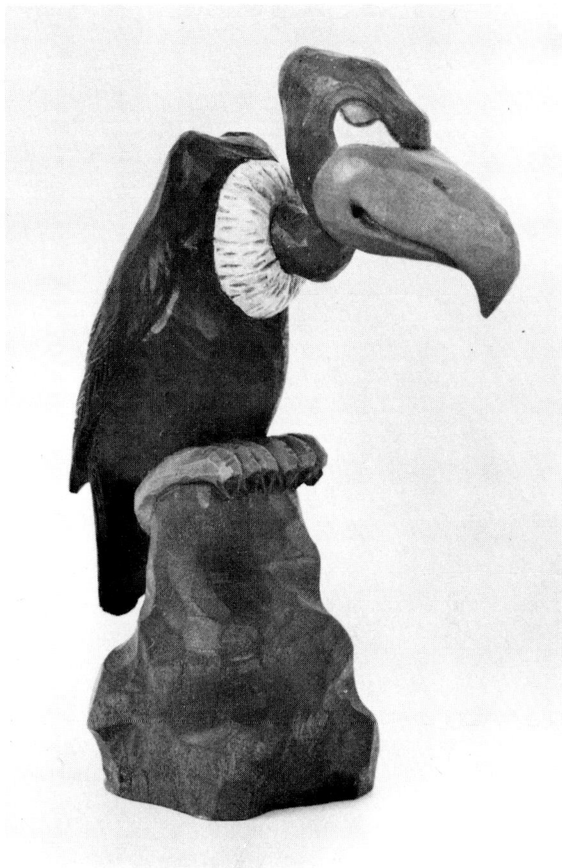

Figure 7 — Finished Buzzard

BLOCKING OUT

Select a nice piece of basswood, 1 3/4 inches thick, 5 inches wide, and 6 inches long. Trace the pattern from the book and transfer it to the block of basswood, making sure the grain runs up and down the 6″ length of wood. Use a band saw or coping saw to cut out the side view. (Fig. 8)

Next, draw the front and back view on the project. Darkening, with a lead pencil, the area of wood to be removed, making it easier to understand the exact amount of wood to be taken off. (Fig. 9) Carefully carve away the black areas, starting with the sides of the head. Be careful not to put too much pressure on the cuts as the neck will break away easily. The head should now be about 1″ thick, making the bill narrow at the point. You can now block out the body, removing the areas of darkened wood from the sides until you have the desired thickness of the body, leaving the feet the full width of the material for now. (Fig. 10)

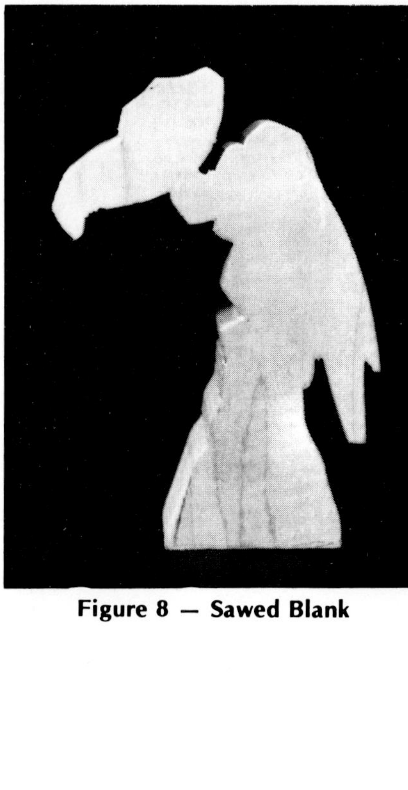

Figure 8 — Sawed Blank

To rough out the thickness of the base, make a small cut just under the bottom of the feet. Using a 12mm gouge, remove wood from the upper sides of the base until it is about 1″ thick. The bottom of the base will be 1 3/4 inches thick, which is the full thickness of the material.

To get the proper thickness of the feet, start with a center line and draw three claws on each foot. Each claw is about 3/16 of an inch wide. Then remove the remaining excess wood from the sides of the claws.

Next, draw a curved line around the back of the bill and remove about 1/8 inch of wood from each side of the head only. Do not remove any wood from the sides of the bill at this time. It is to be wider than the head. The back part of the head should now be about 3/4″ wide, tapering to a knob on top. More wood can now be removed from the neck. This is a delicate step, and care must be taken to avoid decapitation. The neck should be about 3/8″ wide.

Buzzards have a sprinkling of white pin feathers around the neck, close to the body. The height of

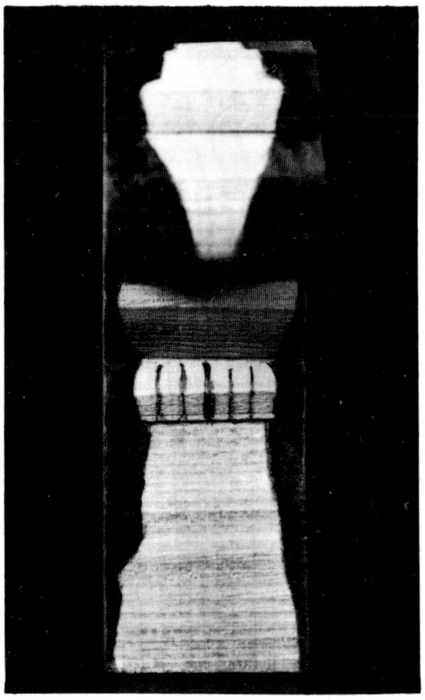
Figure 9

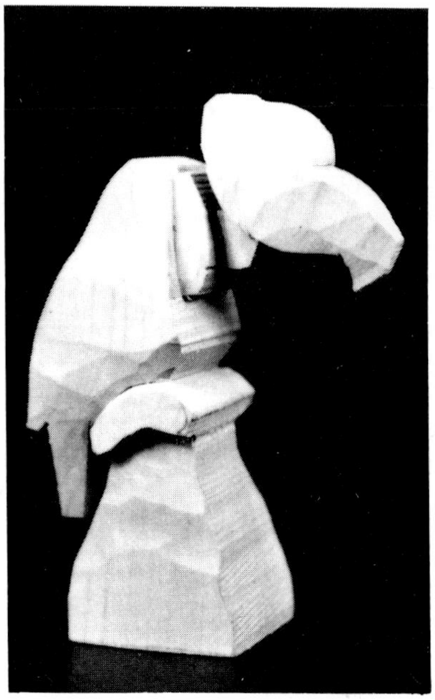
Figure 10

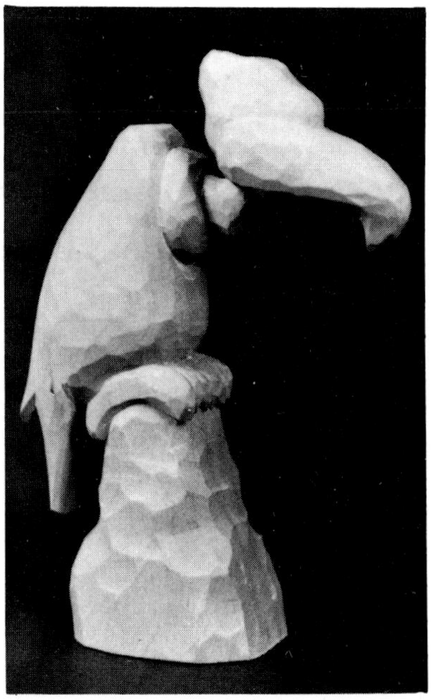
Figure 11

these were pre-cut when the blank was sawed. You must now remove some wood from the sides to get the proper thickness. These feathers look like a collar, about 1'' tall and 1'' wide, through which the buzzard's neck protrudes.

You now have a blocked-out buzzard with all dimensions of head, body, and base thickness established. (Fig. 10) The next step involves rounding up the figure and applying the small details.

ROUNDING

Begin by rounding off the square edges or corners, which run up and down the back. Then round up the stomach between the neck and feet. Once the body is satisfactory, round up the edges of the small collar around the neck. Next, round the neck very carefully, then finish up the back of the head and bill.

Returning to the feet, use a v-tool and carve a line between each toe. You should now have three blocky or square-looking toes on each foot. Take your knife and round these, putting sharp claws on the ends of each toe.

Round off the corners of the base only roughly. These should be left looking rugged and rocky, with a few cracks and crevices added with a v-tool or small gouge. (Fig. 11)

DETAILING

Once the buzzard is rounded into its desired shape, draw on the mouth and eyes, referring to the drawing or finished photo as a guide. Use a 3mm v-tool to carefully carve these facial details. (Fig. 7) Tiny holes, for skin texture, are made in the top of the head with an ice pick or awl.

Next, draw the feathers and wing detail on the bird. Use a 6mm v-tool to carve the outlines of the feathers, and a 3mm v-tool to add the small lines or final feather texture.

Still using your 3mm v-tool, create tiny feathers around the collar by making very small cuts — toward the center of the collar where the neck emerges.

FINISHING

Using 220 grit sandpaper, sand lightly to remove burrs and splinters. The buzzard is now ready to paint. Some carvers like to put a sealer on the project first, using 1/2 shellac and 1/2 denatured alcohol. Let dry thoroughly. I prefer to paint directly on the wood, using acrylic paints, thinned with water.

COLORS: The buzzard's head and neck are red. His eyes are white and green. The collar is white, and the body is black. The same gold is used for the bill and feet. Claws are black. The buzzard's perch can be brown or grey.

When thoroughly dry, I apply a thin coat of hand-rubbed Provincial Umber Antiquing Toner. Let dry, and then wax.

BOTTOMLAND FARMER

Along the headwaters of the Osage River on Tebo Creek, prior to the building of Truman Dam, there were many acres of rich, fertile, bottom farm land. It took a special breed of farmer to work this land for, year after year, nearly half the crops were lost to floodwaters. Still, year after year, the bottomland farmer refused to quit.

One such farmer I have always admired is an uncle of mine who farmed river bottomland for many years. Planting his crops every spring, he never failed to believe that this year would yield the biggest harvest ever.

Another winter has passed. It's time to sharpen the old plowshare and try again.

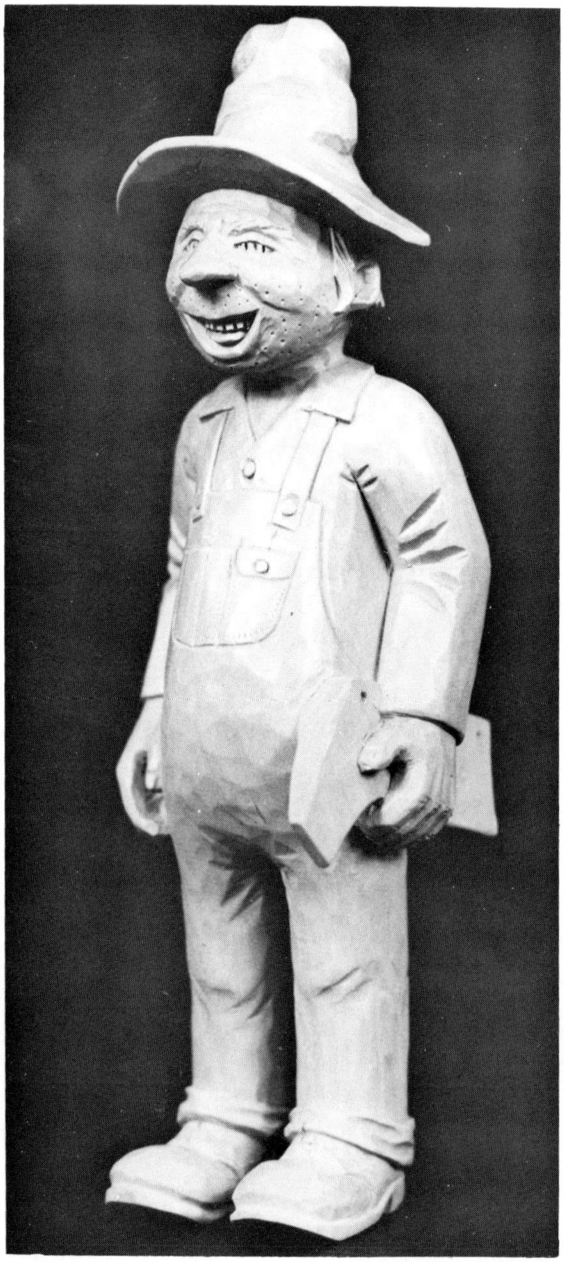

Figure 12 — Finished Farmer

BLOCKING OUT

To carve your farmer, trace the pattern and transfer it to a piece of basswood, 3'' X 3'' X 8''. Cut out the side view with a band saw or coping saw. (Fig. 13)

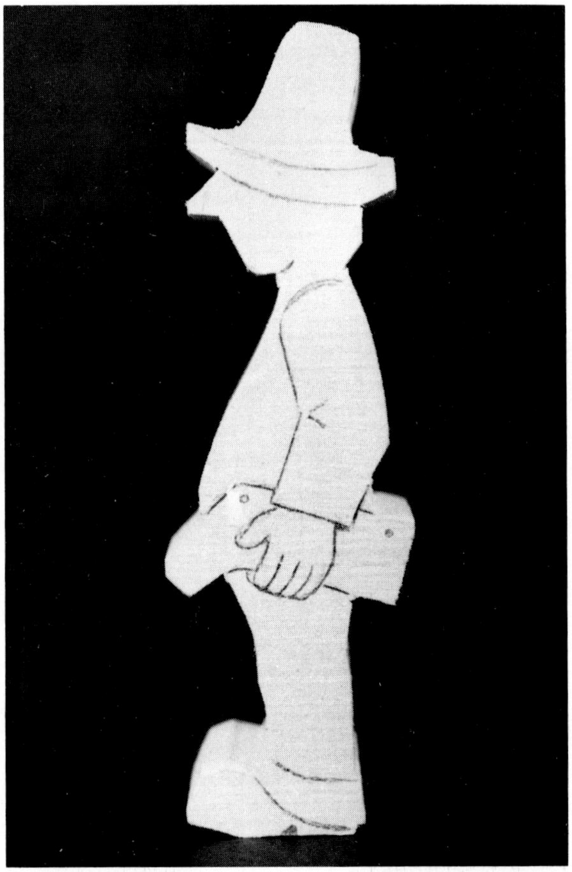

Figure 13 — Sawed Blank For The Farmer

Not all farmers plant row crops. By replacing the plowshare with a hay fork or scoop shovel, you can create a cattle or hog farmer. Add a garden hoe for a vegetable farmer, or use your imagination to design other variations.

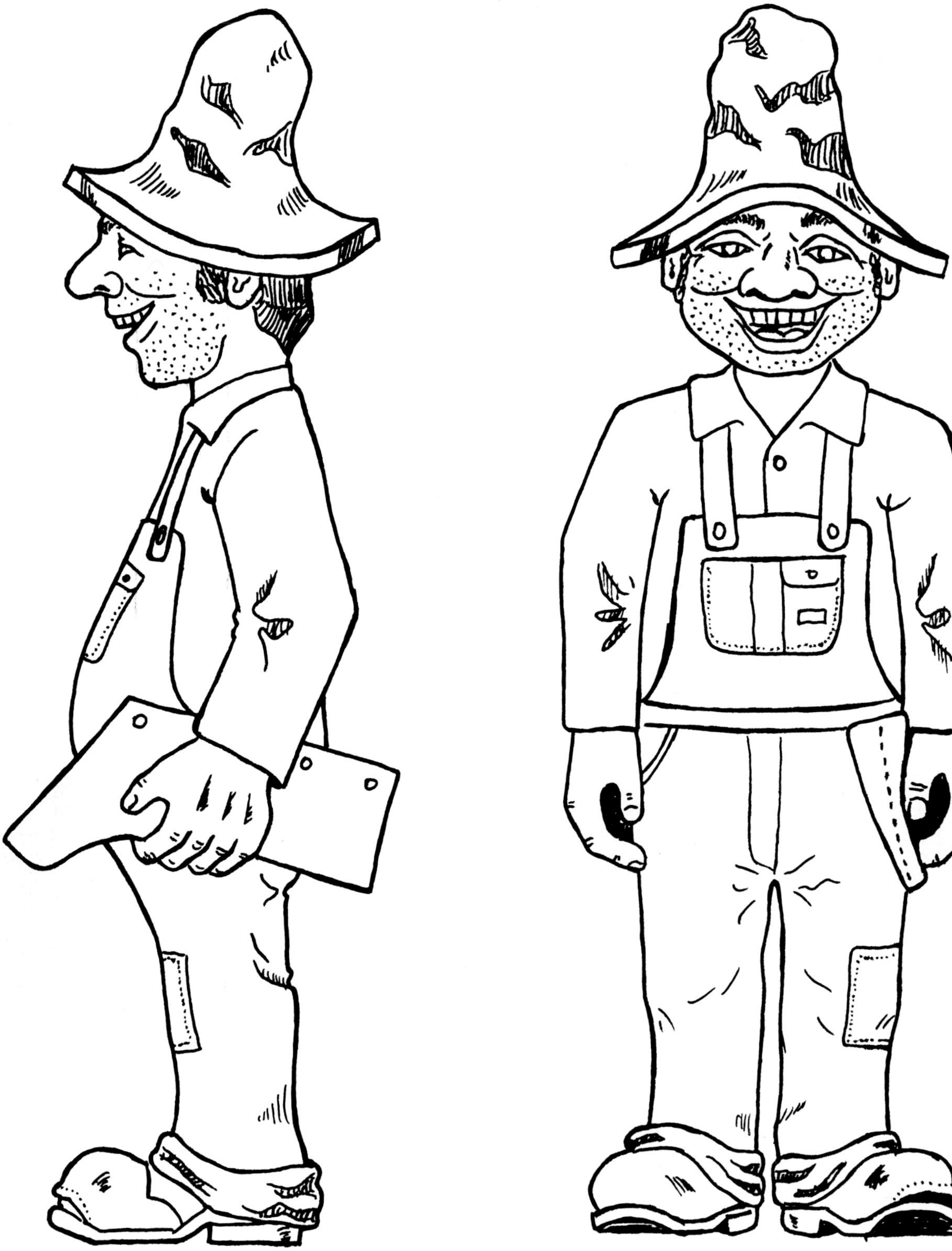

Figure 14 — Pattern for The Bottomland Farmer

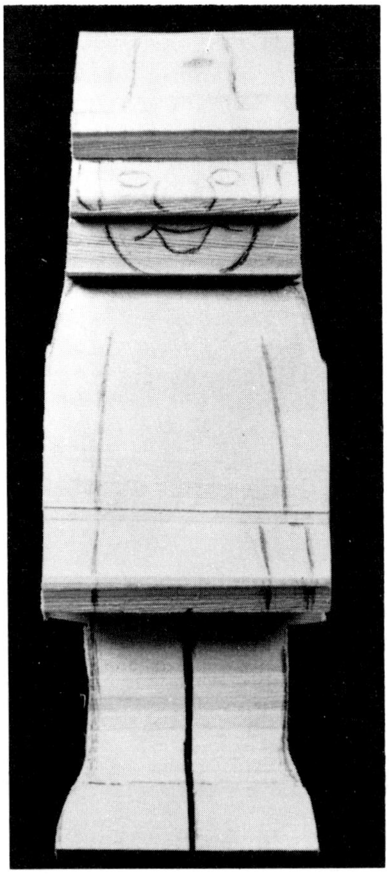

Figure 15

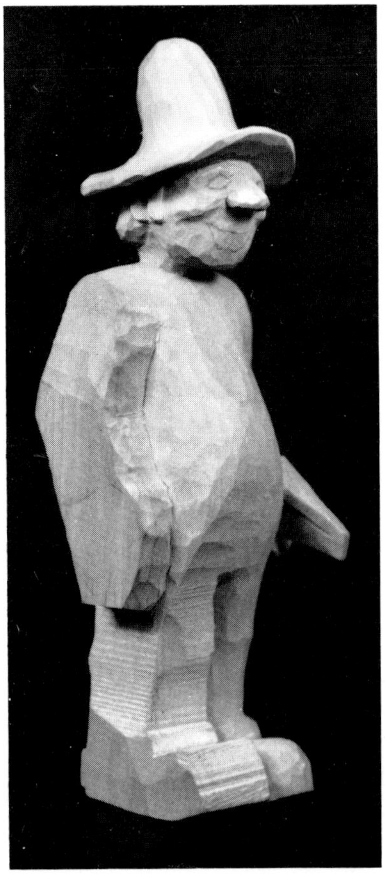

Figure 16

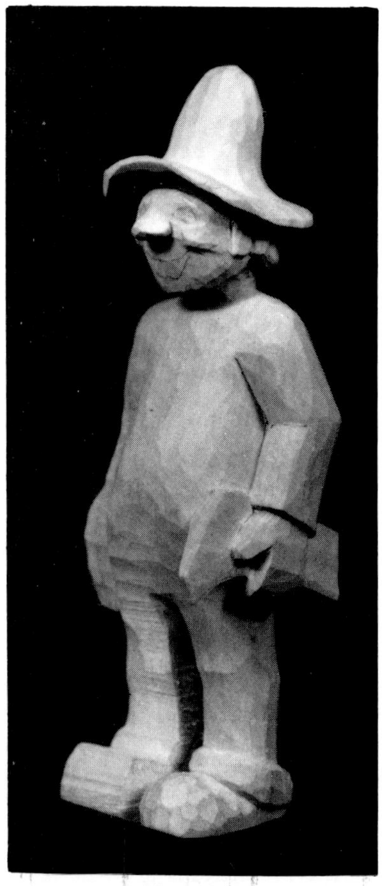

Figure 17

To carve the farmer with a plowshare, draw on the front view as shown in Fig. 15, using care to draw the width of the left hand holding the plowshare.

Laying the figure on its back, saw out the front view, removing wood along the sides and the legs. Make a small cut between the legs. Taper the shoulders gradually, being careful not to remove too much wood from the hat and head as this area will be shaped by whittling.

Using your knife, begin carving the figure by removing the remaining excess wood on each side of the hat and head. When the correct width has been reached for the hat brim, make a cut around the upper edge of the brim, and continue removing wood from the crown of the hat. When the crown is completed, make a cut around the lower edge of the hat brim and remove wood from the sides of the face between the lower edge of the hat brim and the shoulders. Leave a bulge on each side of the head for ears.

Finish blocking out the head by using a small gouge to remove excess wood from each side of the nose. Then, with your knife, remove excess wood around the neck and under the ears until the neck is the right size.

Continuing on to the body, establish the dimensions of the plowshare by using a large gouge to remove excess wood in front of the right hand, across the stomach, and along the right-hand side of the plowshare. (Fig. 16) Using your knife, round out the left hand and remove a small amount of wood from the left side of the plowshare. The left thumb is resting on the plowshare, while the fingers are curled under the bottom edge. (Fig. 17) If your farmer is not to be holding a plowshare, carve a clutched fist and drill a hole for his shovel or hay fork.

The next step in blocking out the body involves using a gouge to remove excess wood from the front of the arms and along each side of the stomach and chest. The dimensions of the legs and feet were established when the front and side views were sawed out. If they match the pattern correctly, they will need little roughing out.

Continue using your gouge to rough out the farmer's back side. Remove the excess wood from the seat of his pants, and flatten his back between his elbows and shoulder blades. Finally, complete the blocking-out process by removing a small area of wood behind the right hand.

ROUNDING THE FARMER

Now that all dimensions of height width, and thickness are established, it is time to do the actual rounding up of the figure. Although this can begin anywhere, I usually start by rounding the crown of the hat. Smooth up and round the corners and edges of the hat brim, then proceed to the head. (If you have little or no experience carving faces, it might be helpful at this point to consult Harold Enlow's book on carving faces and expressions.)

Round up the nose. Take a small gouge and make two indentations for the eyes. Using the same gouge, make a slight cut under the cheeks, starting at the nose and curving outward. This sets the facial lines in a smiling position. With a dark pencil, draw on an open and laughing mouth and two open eyes. These will be carved later with the final detailing.

To carve the ears and sideburns, draw them on with a dark pencil, outline them with a small v-tool, and round up the corners and edges with your knife. Recess the wood from around the ears and sideburns until they stick out slightly.

When rounding the body, I usually begin with the shoulders and work down, rounding the arms and stomach. Using a v-tool, or the tip of your knife, make a sharp line along the arms where they meet the body. Round up the hands and thumbs, using a small v-tool to cut the grooves between the fingers. Working on down the figure, round up the lower part of his stomach and the seat of his pants. Then round the legs and overall cuffs, finishing up with the feet.

DETAILING THE FARMER

The final details are what actually bring out the personality in a caricature carving. These are very important, and sharp tools are an absolute necessity.

Begin detailing by putting large wrinkles on the hat. A small v-tool is then used to texture the hair and sideburns. With a 3mm gouge, scoop out an oval mound for each eye. Use your smallest v-tool to make two cuts across each mound, forming the eyelids. With a sharp, pointed knife, remove a very thin layer of wood between the eyelids, getting slightly deeper in each corner of each eye. Use an ice pick or awl to punch a small hole for the pupil, then scratch a tiny vertical line on each side of the pupil to form the eyeball. The eyebrows are then carved with your smallest v-tool.

To carve the laughing mouth, which was drawn on earlier, use the pattern as a guide. With a 6mm v-tool, make a cut across the upper lip and a cut across the lower lip. These cuts meet at the corners of the mouth. Use the tip of a sharp knife to remove a shallow layer of wood from the inside of the mouth, making the corners slightly deeper. Then make a cut, horizontally, across the center of the mouth.

This leaves two small bodies of wood inside the mouth. The upper body of wood is separated with several small vertical cuts, forming teeth. Round the corners and edges of the lower body of wood to create the impression of a small tongue. To complete the mouth, use a deep 2mm gouge to carve a line running parallel to, and just under, the lower lip.

The texture of the whiskers is achieved by making tiny punctures with a small v-tool or awl.

When detailing the body, I find it easier to make the collar first, using a small v-tool, then I add the overall straps and bib. The bib has small pockets with tiny stitches made with an awl or pounce wheel. The overall buttons are tiny circles made by rotating the tip of a small gouge or nail set.

The farmer has straps on the back of his overalls, a patch on the seat of his pants, and one on his knee. Use a large v-tool to carve wrinkles where the arm bends in front of the elbow, and where the leg bends behind the knee. With the same tool, cut wrinkles in the cuffs of his overall legs.

If you want your farmer to wear worn-out shoes, cut an opening in the toe of one shoe and add a few rounded toes inside. Use a small v-tool to make the shoe soles.

Put the finishing touches on the fingers by carving small knuckles and fingernails.

Apply two tiny bolt holes along the top edge of the plowshare.

I finish my farmer by waxing with a good grade of paste wax and buffing lightly when dry.

FANCY DAN

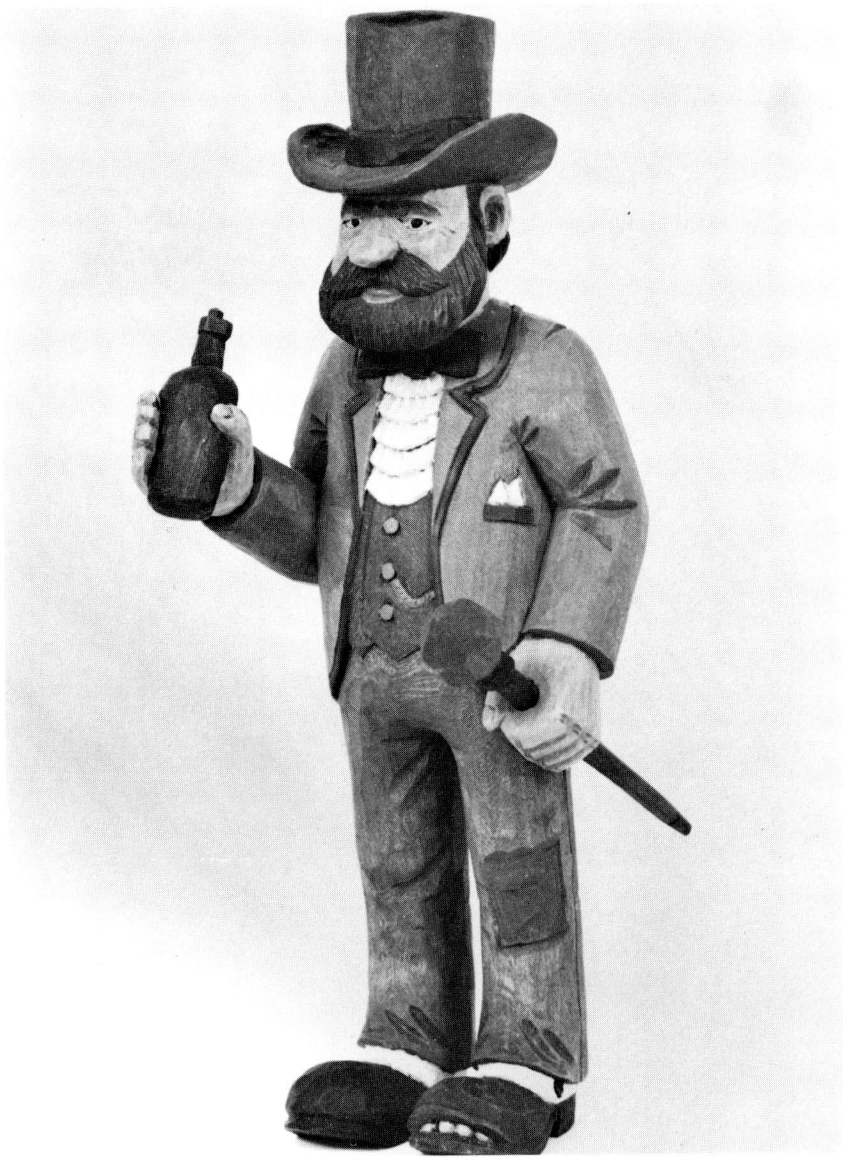

Figure 18 — Fancy Dan Carved and Painted

He first came to this area wearing a suit of flashy Eastern clothes. Driving a brightly painted, horse-drawn peddler's wagon, he traveled from community to community, hawking his snake oil. Promising to cure whatever ailed you, grow hair on the baldest head, and shine the rustiest doorknob, this fellow was undoubtedly one of the first businessmen in this area.

Today, the peddler's wagon has been replaced with large chain stores and plush downtown offices. He may be selling anything from real estate to used cars. Watch out for Fancy Dan. There may be one in your town.

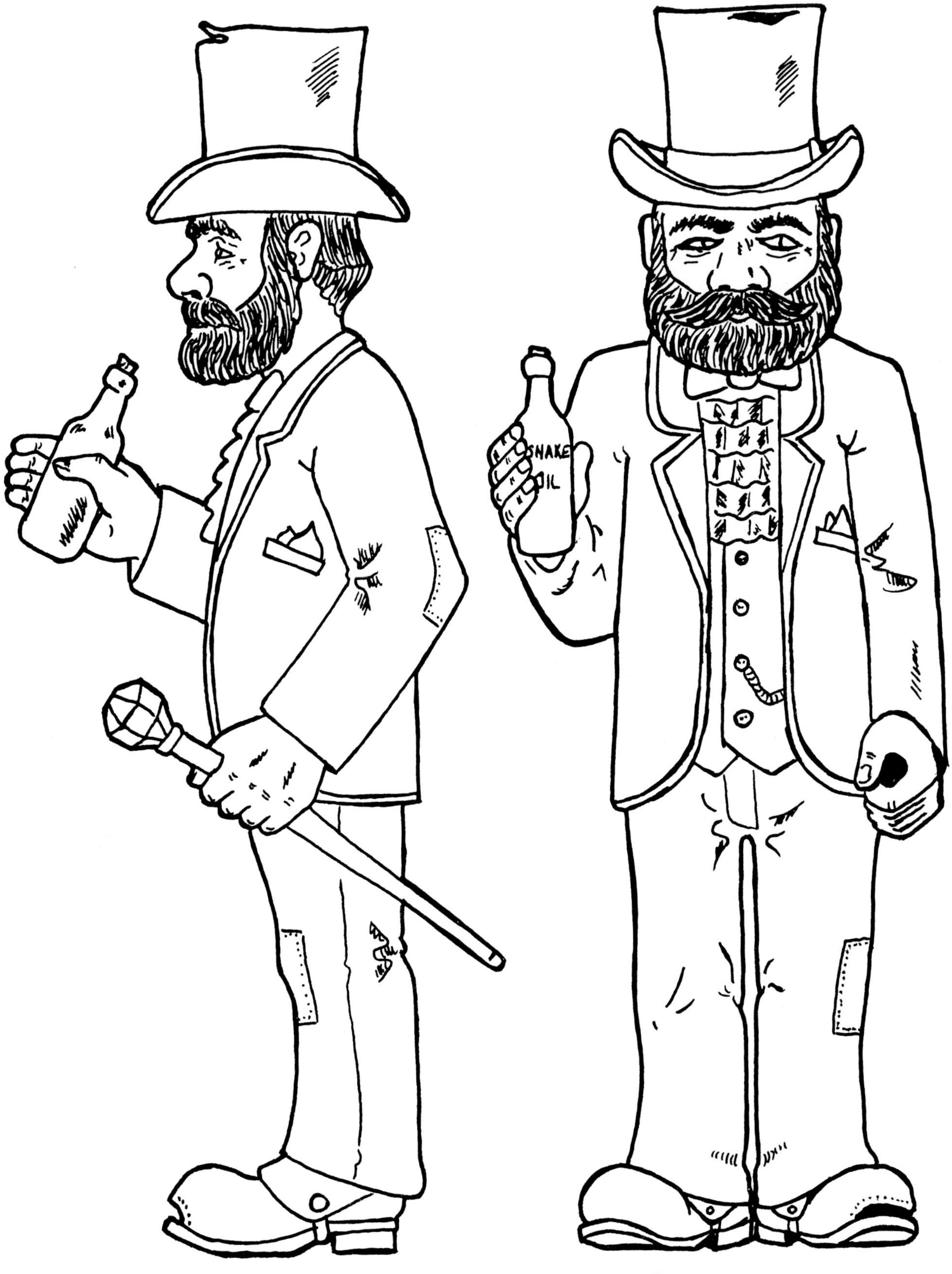

Figure 19 — Pattern for Fancy Dan

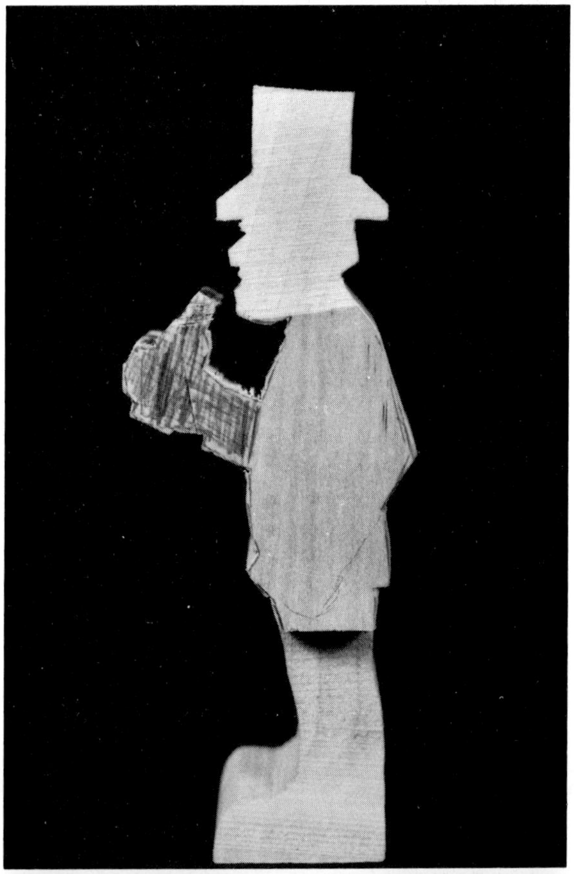

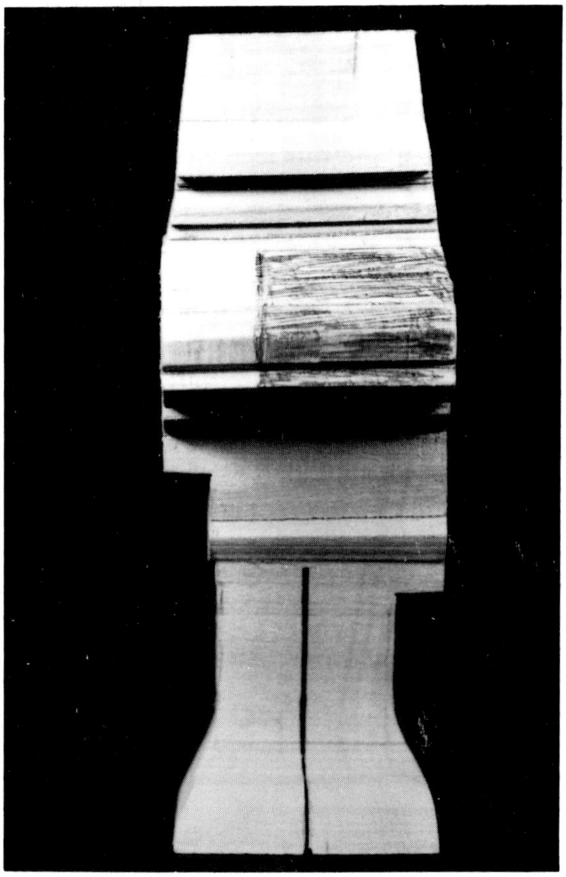

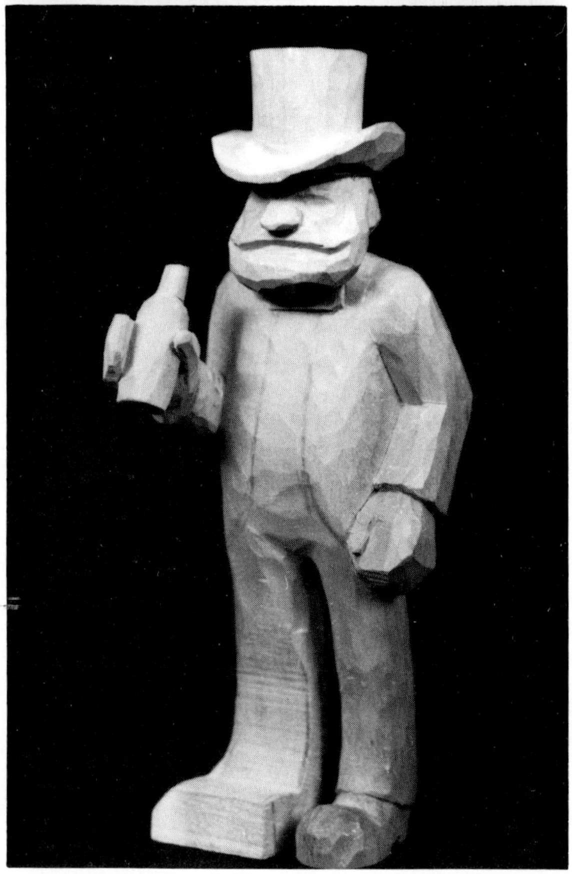

Figures 20, 21, 22

CARVING FANCY DAN

The procedure for carving Fancy Dan is much the same as for the farmer. The pattern is transferred to basswood, and the side and front views are then cut out with a band saw. (Fig. 20 & 21)

I use my knife for blocking out the head, and a large gouge to remove the excess wood from the right hand. Once all the desired widths and thicknesses for the entire figure have been established, the carving can be rounded in the same manner as the farmer. (Fig. 22)

Fancy Dan's clothes make him a very enjoyable carving to detail — tears and patches add character, while his top hat and lace shirt suggest that he truly is a gentleman.

The lace on the shirt is carved with a 2mm gouge. The beard texture is achieved through the use of a 3mm v-tool. The walking stick is carved separately and inserted through a hole in the hand.

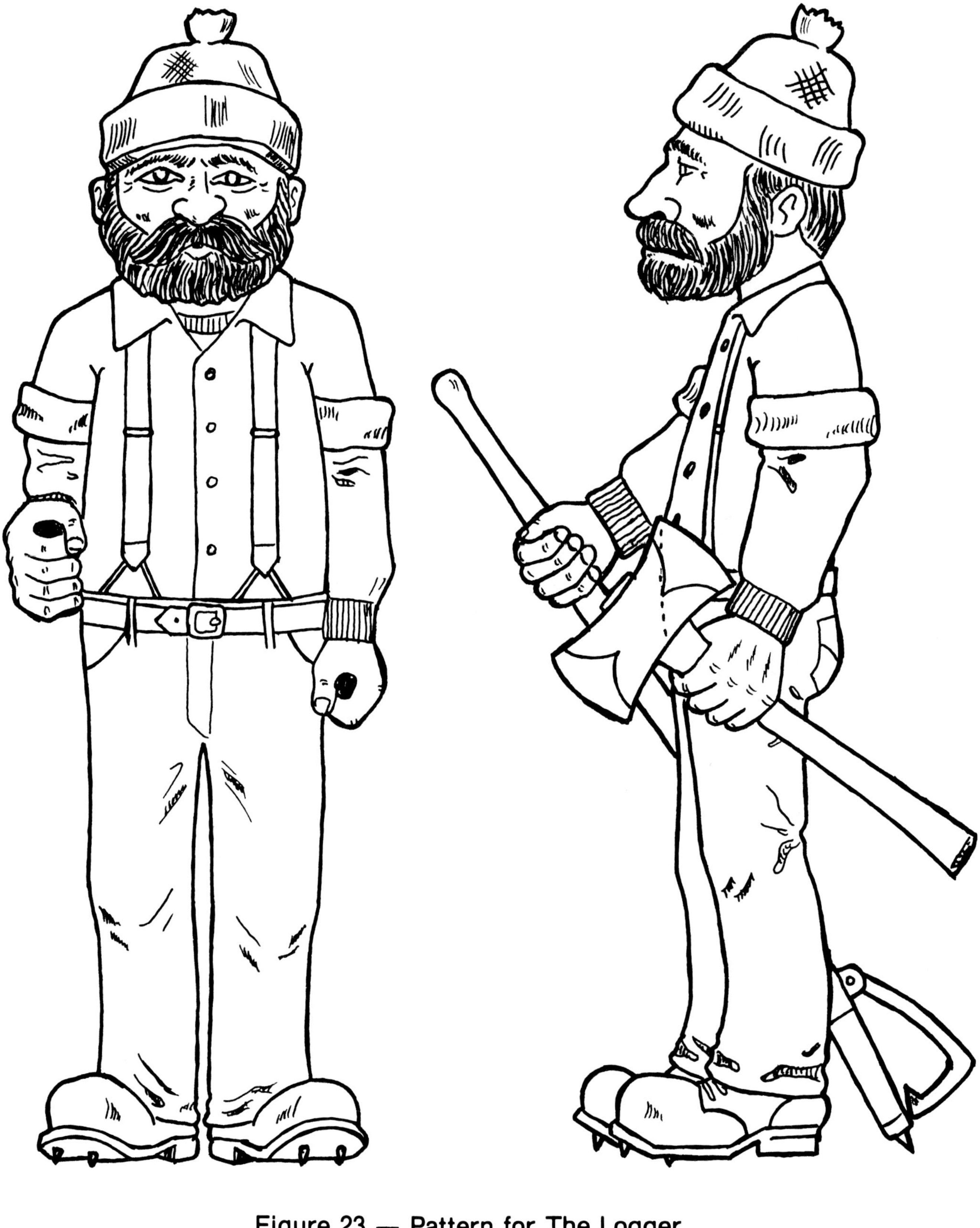

Figure 23 — Pattern for The Logger

THE LOGGER

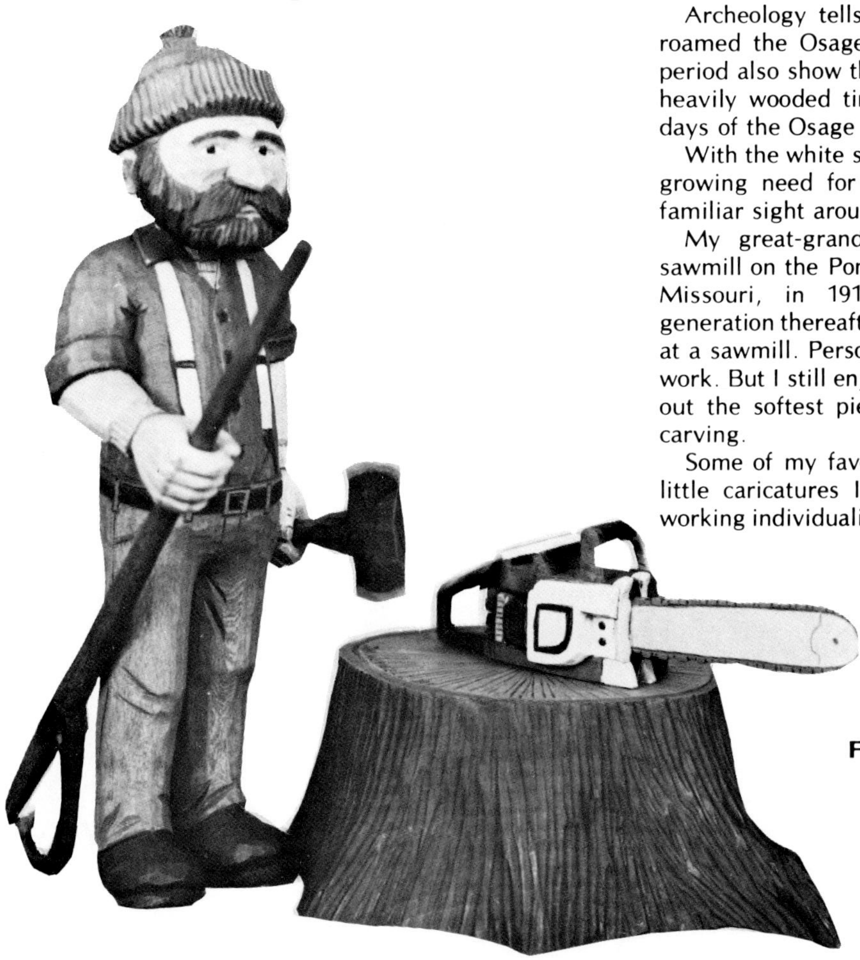

Figure 24 — Logger and Saw

Archeology tells us that great mastodons once roamed the Osage River Basin. Fossils from this period also show that the Truman Lake area was a heavily wooded timberland up to and during the days of the Osage Indian.

With the white settler, in the mid 1850's, came a growing need for lumber. Sawmills were soon a familiar sight around the new communities.

My great-grandfather owned and operated a sawmill on the Pomme de Terre River at Fairfield, Missouri, in 1912. And Maxwells from each generation thereafter have worked at least part-time at a sawmill. Personally, I never cared for the hard work. But I still enjoy going to the mill where I pick out the softest pieces of basswood to use in my carving.

Some of my favorite carvings are the humorous little caricatures I've patterned after these hard-working individualists, the sawmiller and the logger.

CARVING THE LOGGER

When carving the logger or woodsman, a great deal of extra interest can be added through the base and the tools he works with. I often put this figure on a stump or log and add a chain saw or drinking jug as accessories.

Axes and log hooks are basically all the same. But for accurate detail, I have used an actual chain saw for a model. The ax handle is carved in two separate pieces and joined together inside the left hand, while the log hook is carved as one piece and inserted through a hole in the right hand.

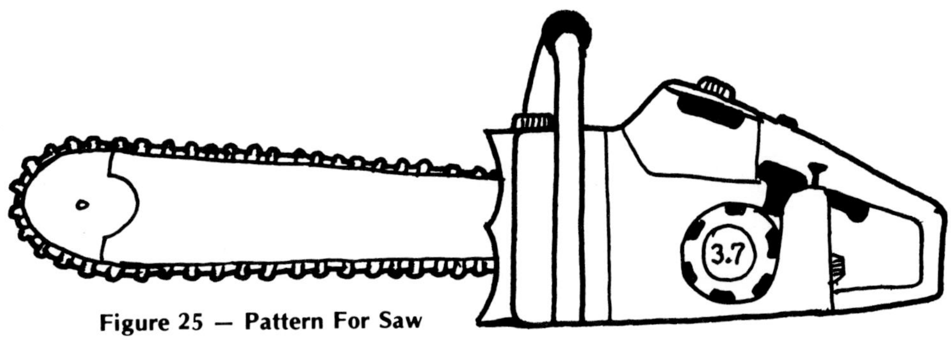

Figure 25 — Pattern For Saw

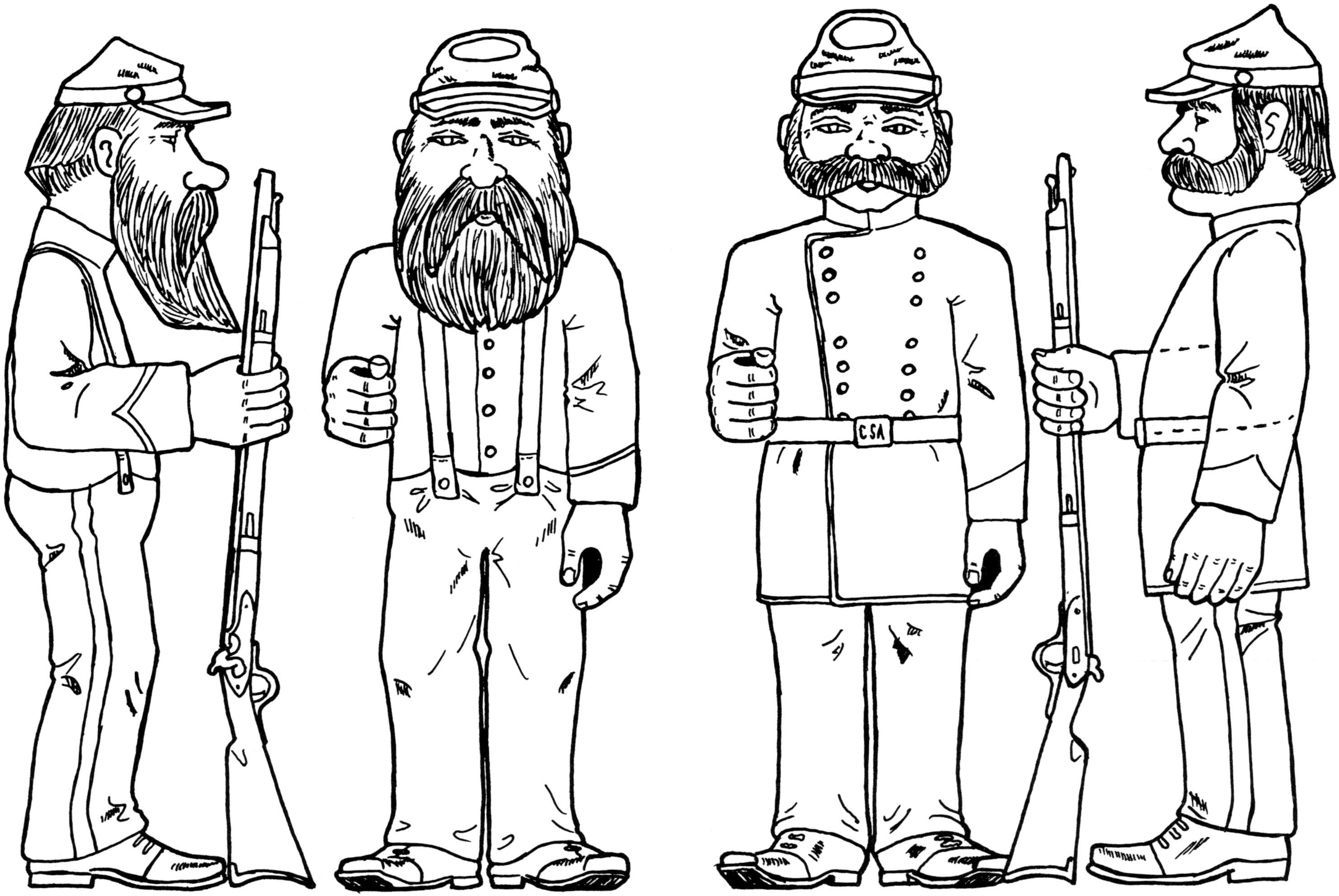

Figure 26 — Pattern for The Yank And Reb

YANK AND REB

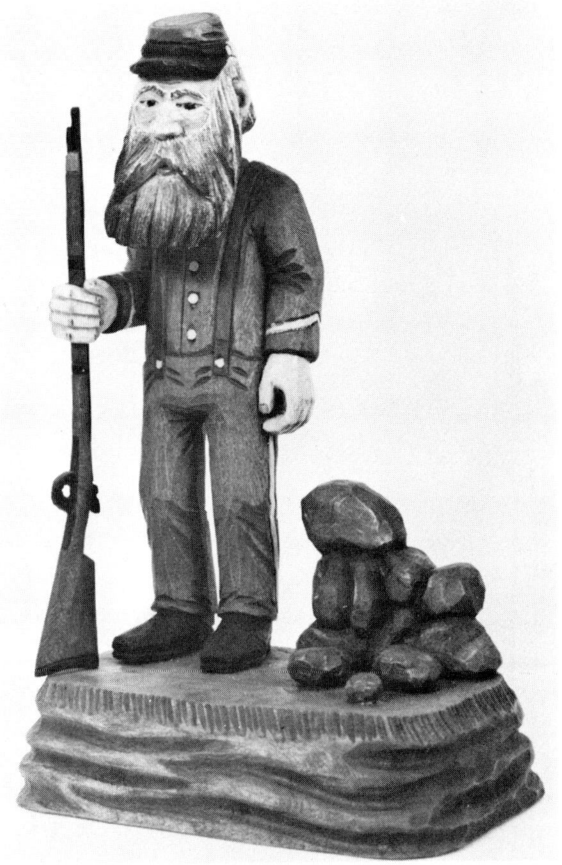

Figure 27 — Yank

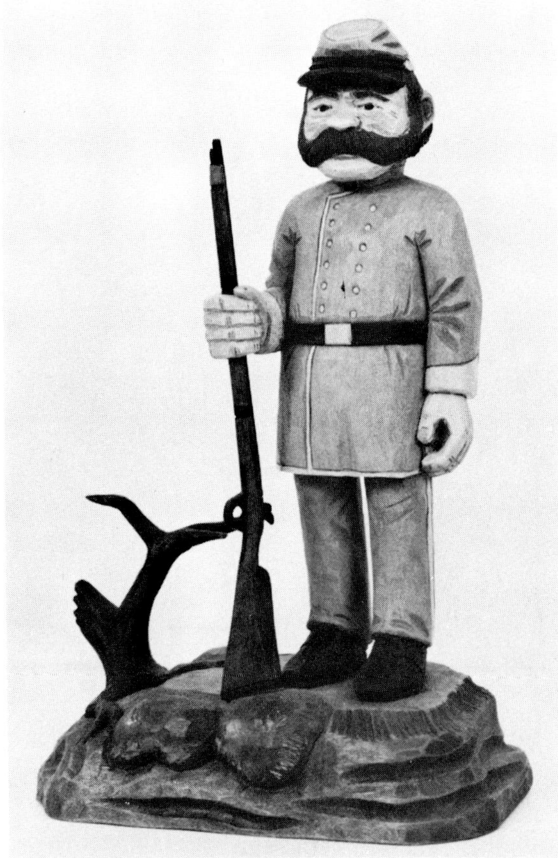

Figure 28 — Reb

Missouri was torn by many battles and skirmishes during the War Between the States. This aspect of my home state's history has always fascinated me, and some of my earliest attempts to create original caricatures depicted Civil War Soldiers.

I soon found that for my carvings to be authentic, a great deal of research into uniforms and equipment was required. Before long, my son, Danny, and I were visiting battlefields in all the Civil-War states.

From our research we learned that there were many variations of the Civil-War uniform. After visiting museums, reading books, and acquiring photographs, I was able to create a soldier that is technically correct down to the number of buttons on his coat, as well as a caricature figure in his whimsical array of garb — bits and pieces of clothing sent from home or picked up on the battlefield.

UNIFORM DETAILS

These figures are both infantrymen. The Yank is carved wearing only his trousers, shirt, and hat, while the Reb proudly sports his official uniform. Their correct colors are blue, trimmed in very light blue, and gray, also trimmed in very light blue. The rifles are carved separately and inserted through a hole in the hand before the figure is attached to the base.

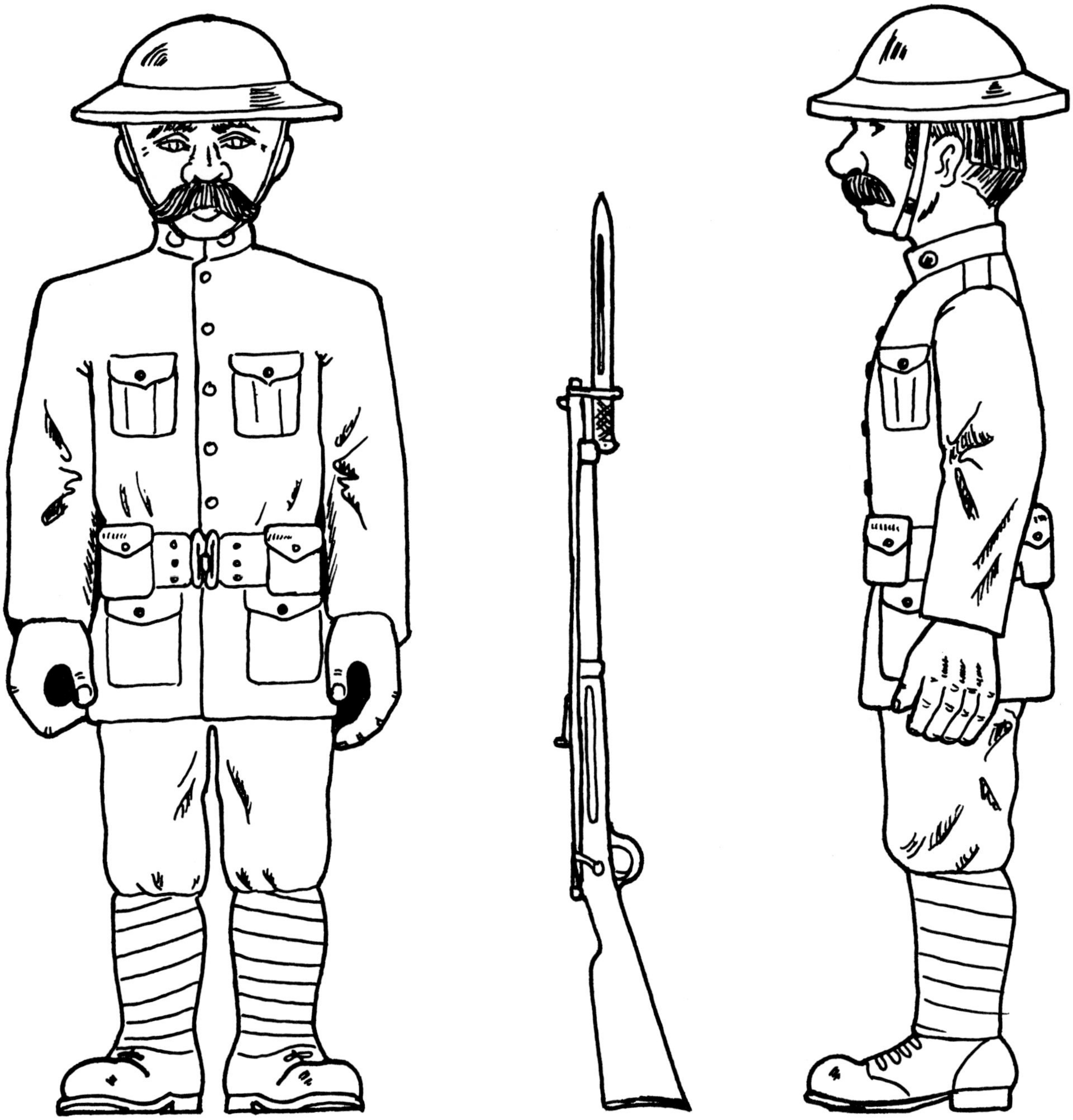

Figure 29 — Pattern for The Doughboy

THE DOUGHBOY

I never had the good fortune to know any Civil War soldiers. But I've known several ''doughboys'', those veterans of the U.S. infantry during World War I who earned their nick-name through a small dried biscuit they carried in their packs and soaked in water to make it edible.

One of the most memorable was an old gentleman who was sitting on the front porch of Parks' General Store in Tightwad, Missouri, cutting a plug of tobacco with a large, bone-handled jackknife. When I commented on the knife's fine workmanship, the seasoned former soldier turned the tool over slowly in his hands and replied, ''Yep . . . Saved my life once, over in France.''

Noting the gleam of interest in my eyes, the old fellow shoved half a plug of tobacco into his mouth and proceeded to tell a tale of enemy lines and German shells in the ''Great War'' of 1918. He and another soldier, so the story went, had crawled under a wagon for cover. A shell hit the wagon and it collapsed on the two soldiers. ''When I came to,'' he recalled, ''my companion was dead, and my own leg was pinned by a wagon timber. Searching for a way out, I found this knife in the dead soldier's pocket and used it to cut the timber and free my leg.''

A true story? Who knows? However, I couldn't help noticing how he favored one leg with a bad limp as he stood up, walked over to the edge of the porch, and spit at the gas pump.

CARVING TIPS

To make my first carved doughboy authentic, I borrowed a complete uniform from a veteran of the First World War.

Additional character can be gained by turning the head slightly and extending the right arm outward so the rifle is held in a vertical position. The bayonet is attached after the rifle is placed through the hand. An attractive base could be added with battlefield obstacles and small bits of tiny braided barbed wire.

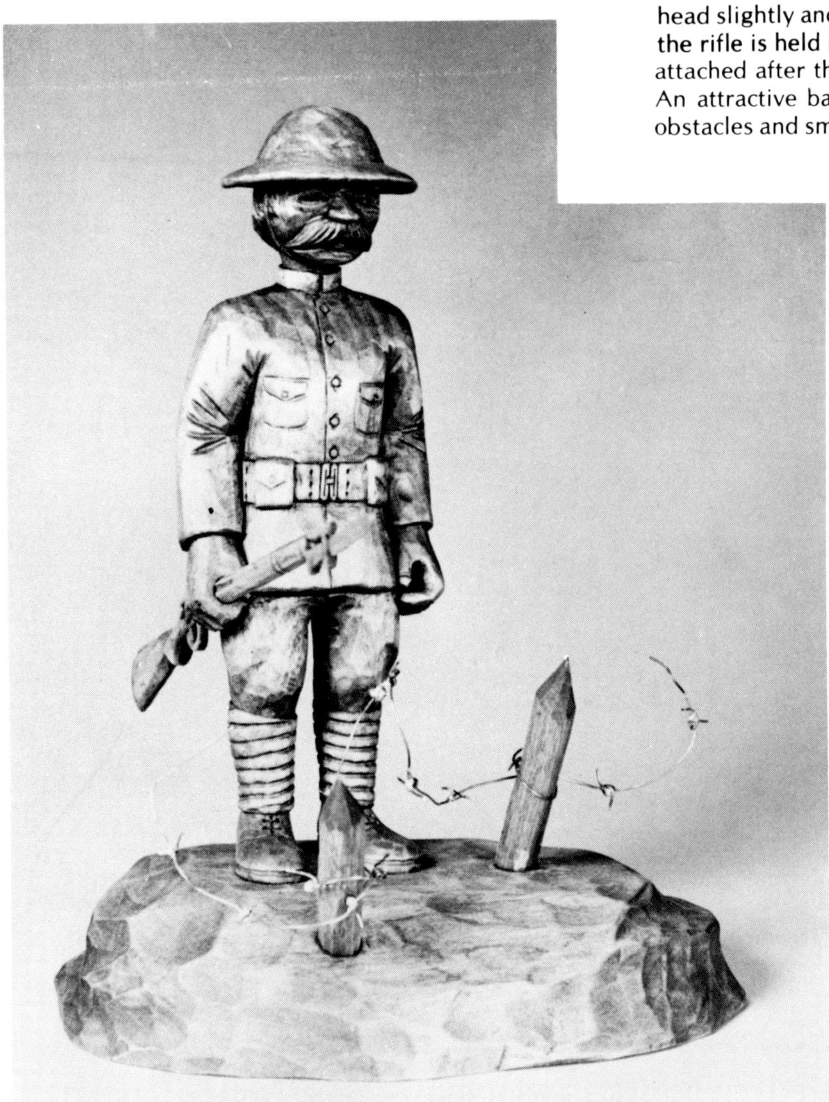

Figure 30 — Doughboy With Battlefield Obstacles And Barbed Wire.

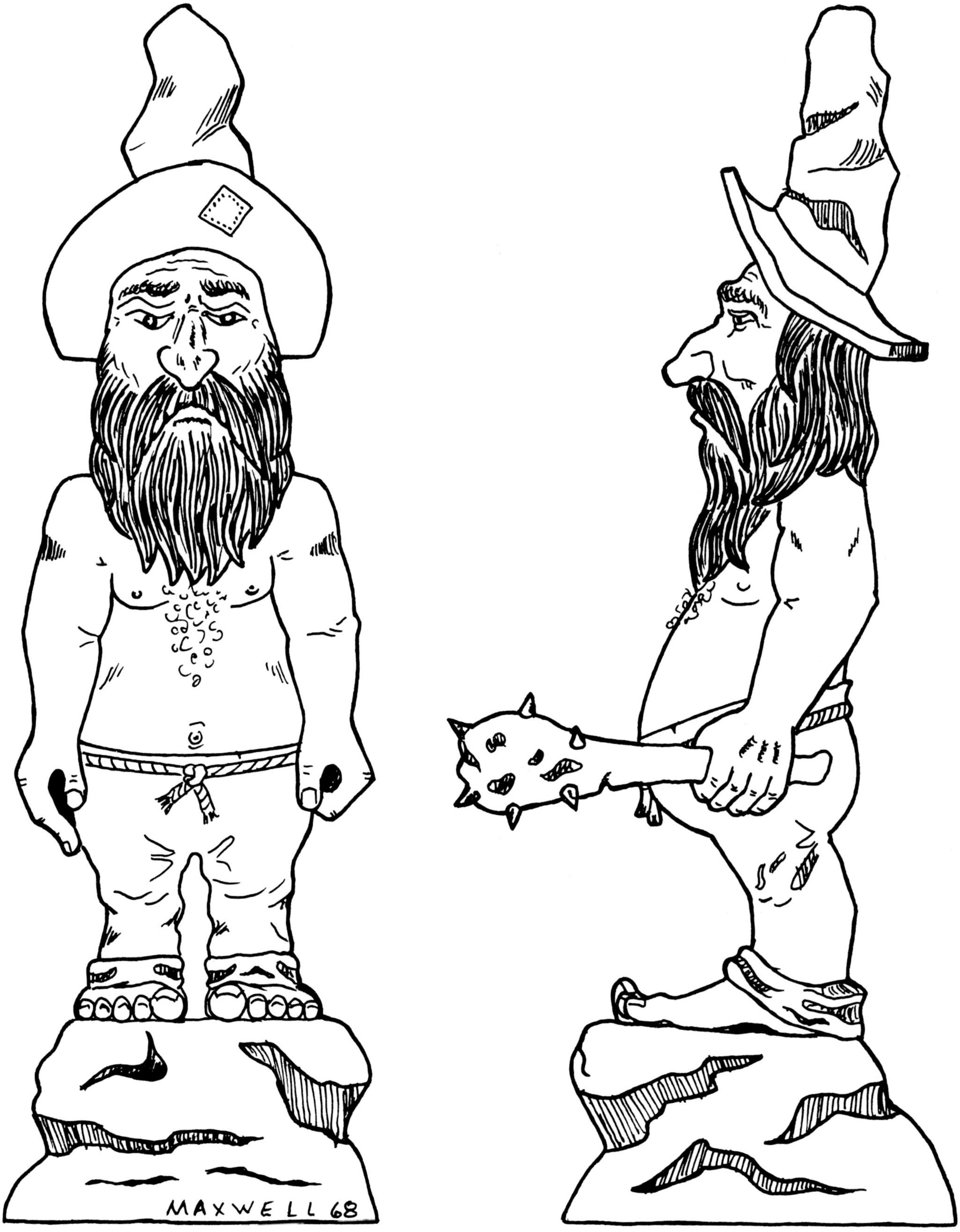

Figure 31 — Pattern for The Swinging Bridge Troll

SWINGING BRIDGE TROLL

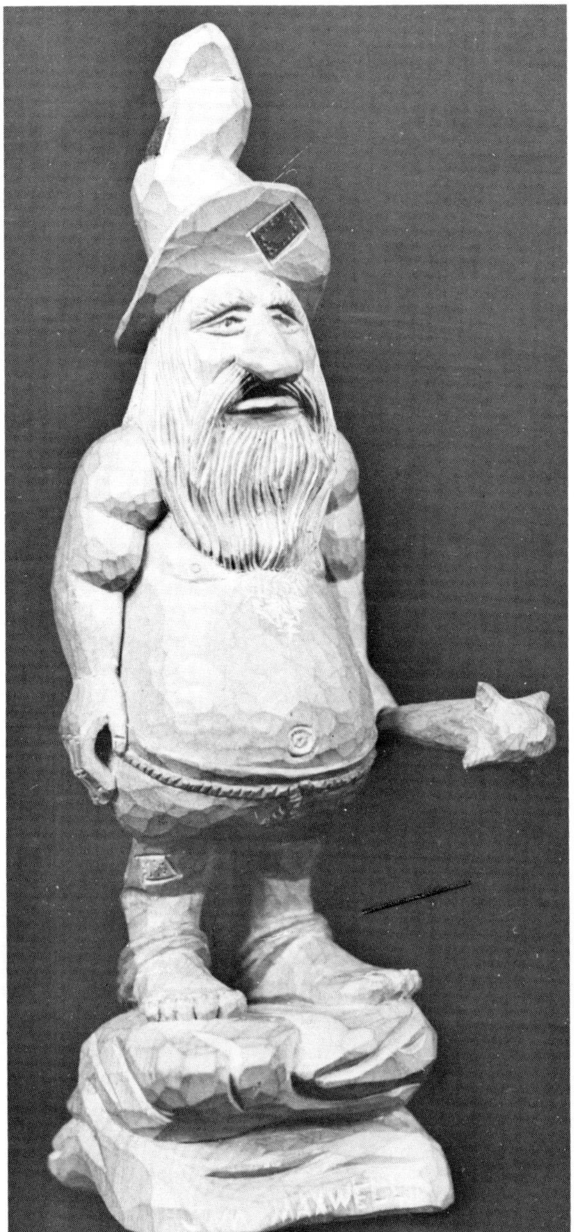

Figure 32 — Swinging Bridge Troll.
Personal Collection
Carved 1968.

A favorite piece of local folklore has to do with the long-span swinging bridges that have dotted the Osage River Basin since the turn of the century. Rumor has it that tiny, troll-like people, ugly by our standards, made their homes under these bridges. With the gradual disappearance of the swinging bridge, this legend has become increasingly difficult to verify.

I, however, am here to testify to the existence of swinging-bridge trolls. It was late one spring evening in 1960. My friend, Danny Chambers, and I were fishing under the swinging bridge at Gray's Ford on Tebo Creek. We sat happily by the fire, keeping an eye on our propped-up poles, and listening to the sounds of the night. Gradually, we became aware of a sound that didn't fit — a strange scratching in the tackle box. Upon investigating, we discovered one of the strangest creatures I have ever seen. A miniature of the crustiest, ugliest, hairiest, and most pot-bellied old man you could imagine. He had apparently climbed in, looking for food or bait, and was trapped. We helped him out and gave him some liquid refreshment. He shared our fire awhile, then went on his way.

Being one of the few people in this area who has actually seen a swinging-bridge troll, I am often questioned as to the exact description of the little creature, and, of course, as to the contents of the jug.

CARVING TIPS

Because swinging bridges provide adequate shelter year-round, my trolls need very little clothing. Their height seldom exceeds six inches, so they often stand on rocks or ledges for improving visibility. The club is for protection from predators. It is carved separately and inserted through a hole in his left hand.

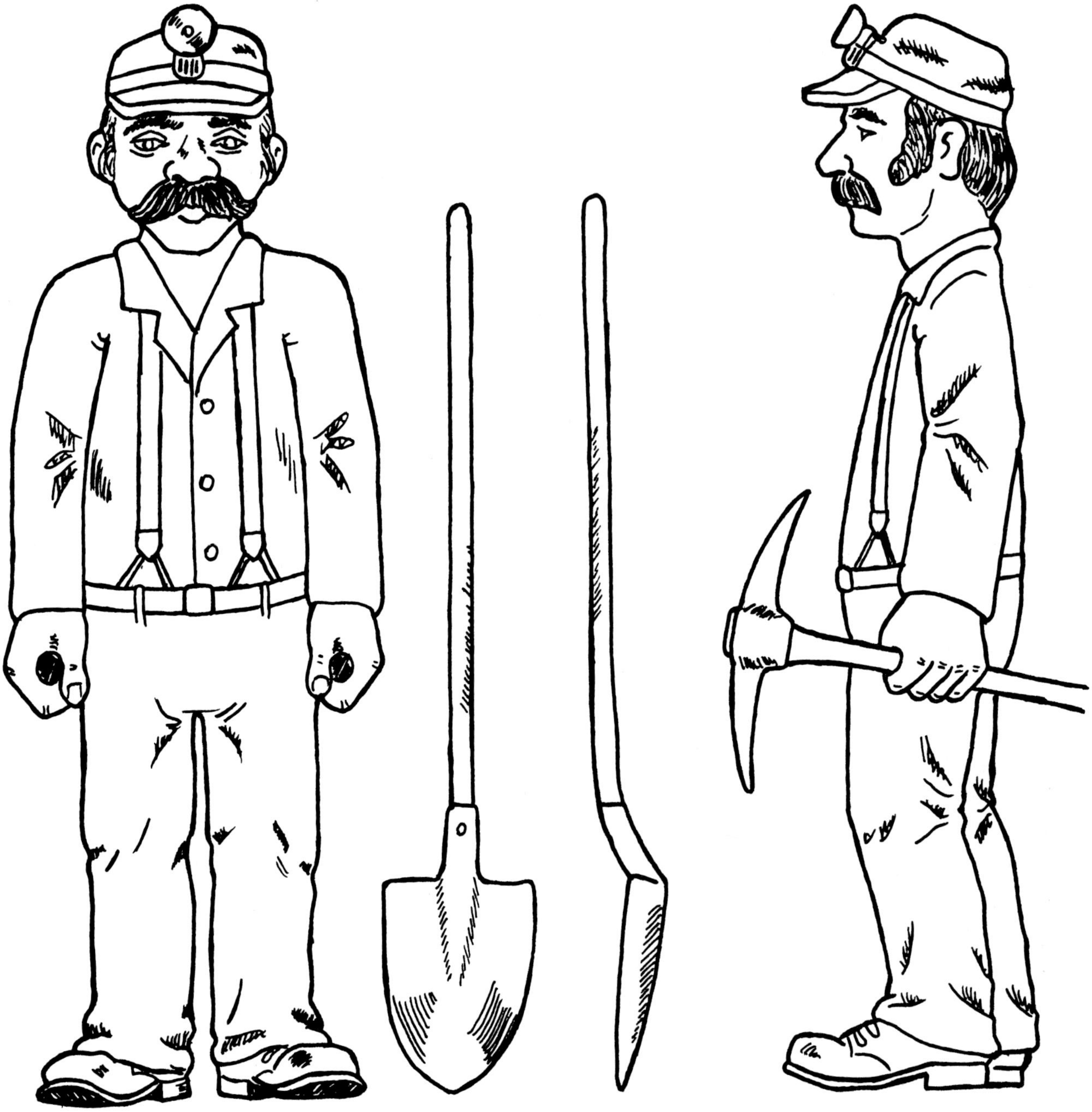

Figure 33 — Pattern for The Coal Miner

COAL MINER

From the Glacial Plains north of the Missouri River, through the Ozark Highlands, Missouri is rich in coal deposits. But in the plains area north of the Osage River, called the Osage Basin after the Indian tribe that had its main settlement there, coal deposits are so near the surface that open strip mining is possible in many places.

The area surrounding my own hometown of Windsor owes a large chunk of its history to the mining of coal. Abandoned strip pits at the edge of town, despite their "no trespassing" signs, are still favorite haunts of fishermen, fossil hunters, and hooky-playing schoolboys in search of a swim.

Over the past hundred years, mining methods have, of course, changed dramatically. The individual miner you might have met on the street some years ago, a pick and shovel in his hands, a carbide light on his hat, and nothing clean but the whites of his eyes, is vanished. He has traded his pick, shovel, and horse-drawn tumblebug for giant excavators, bulldozers, and electric scoops.

But for purposes of this book, our figure represents a miner of the pick-and-shovel era.

CARVING AND PAINTING TIPS

After carving your miner, a realistic effect can be achieved by painting the figure in dull colors and applying a hevy coat of antiquing toner. The pick and shovel are carved separately. The base is carved to look like a large mound of dirt with a few chunks of coal.

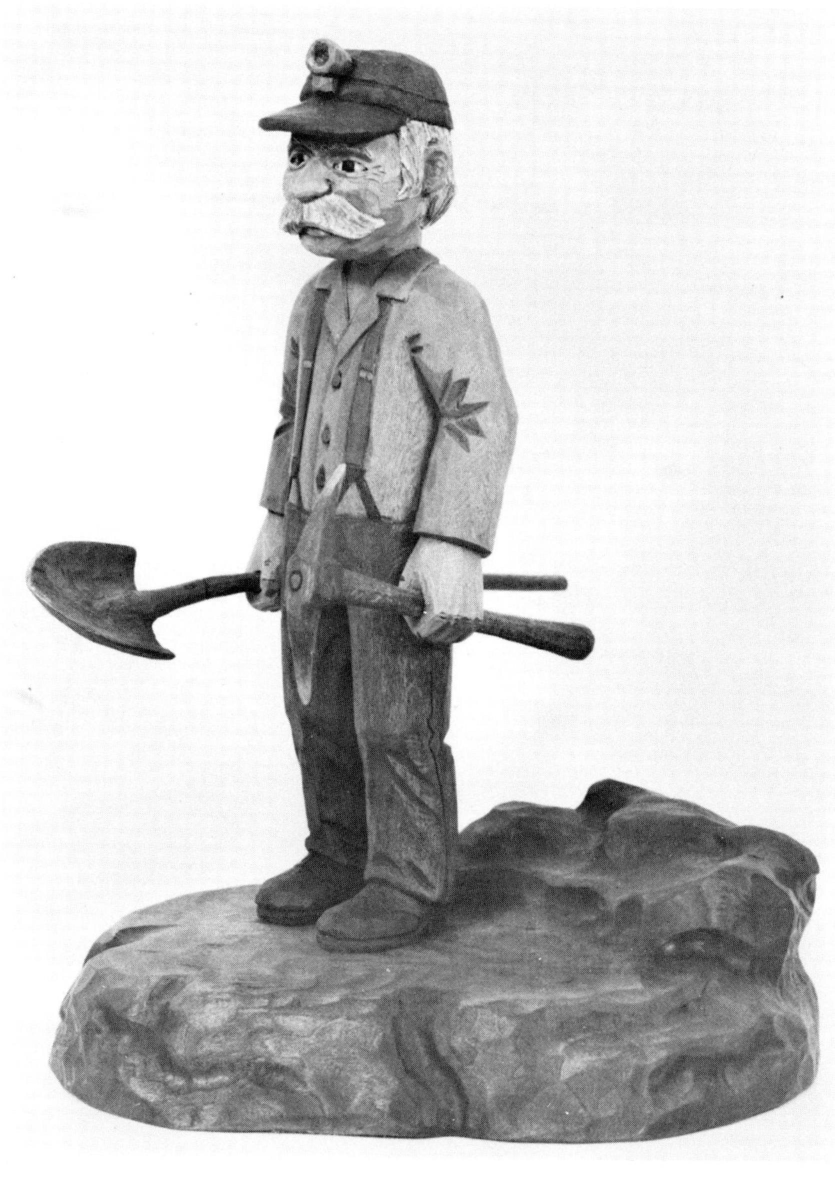

Figure 34 — Completed Coal Miner

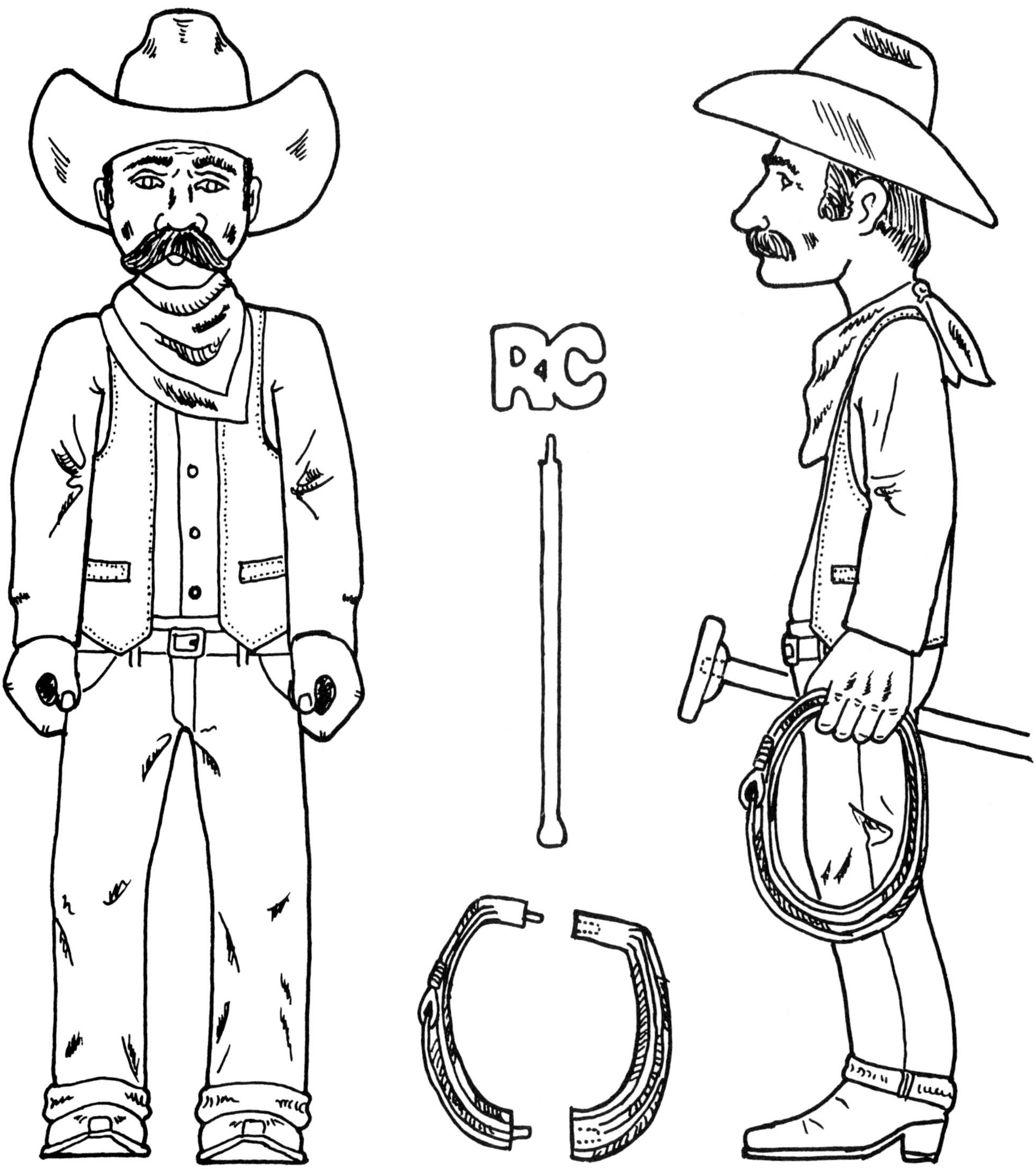

Figure 35 — Pattern for The Cattleman

THE CATTLEMAN

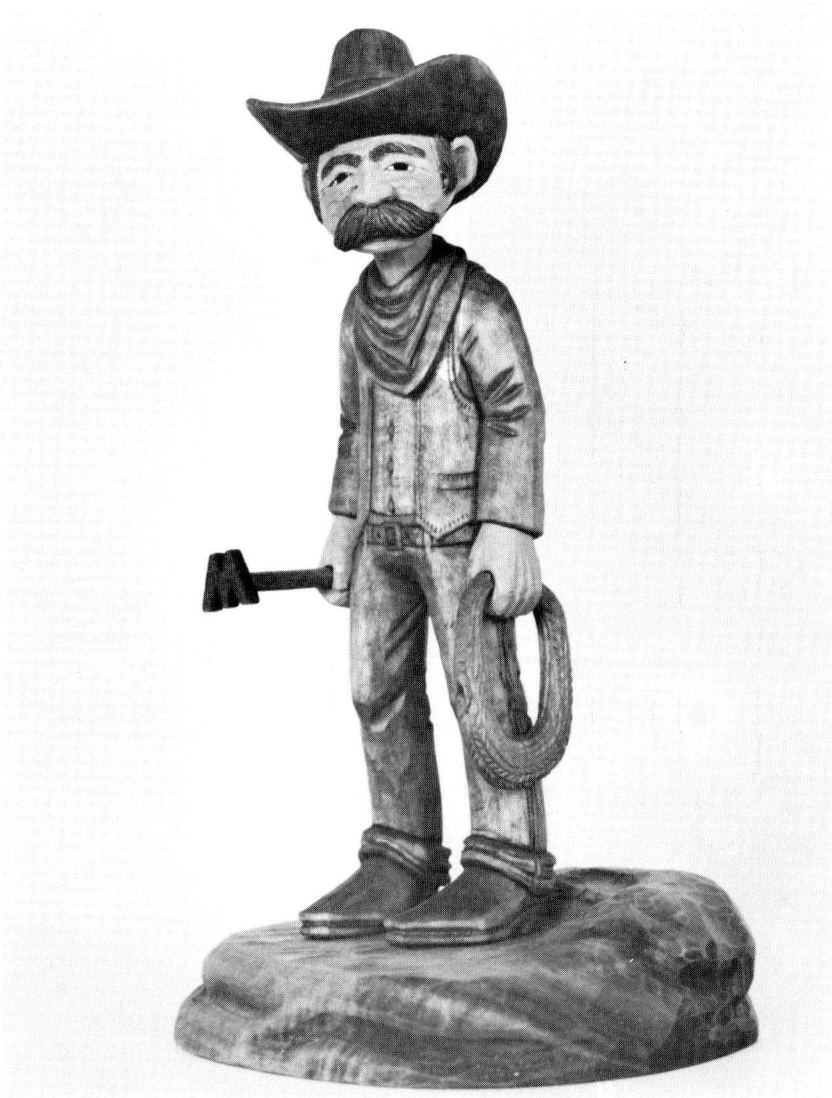

Figure 36 — Cattleman with Personalized Branding Iron.

Cattle are a common sight throughout the hills of Missouri. Whether it's one or two cows in the feed lot, or a herd of hundreds roaming a large and beautiful spread, nearly every farm and ranch in Missouri is somehow involved with cows.

I enjoy watching the cattlemen in my area. Even in these modern times, they still evoke nostalgic thoughts of cowboys of the Old West. With their western boots and wide-brimmed hats, they remind me of western movie heroes I admired as a boy.

The American cowboy has long been a favorite subject for artists and sculptors. This is a cowboy I designed a few years ago. He is enjoyable and easy to carve. And he can be made into a personalized figure by putting the initials or logo of your choice on his branding iron.

CARVING TIPS

In the finished photo, I have used the old Andy Anderson technique of carving the head separately and turning it slightly to the left.

The branding iron and rope are each made in two pieces, inserted through the hands, and then joined together.

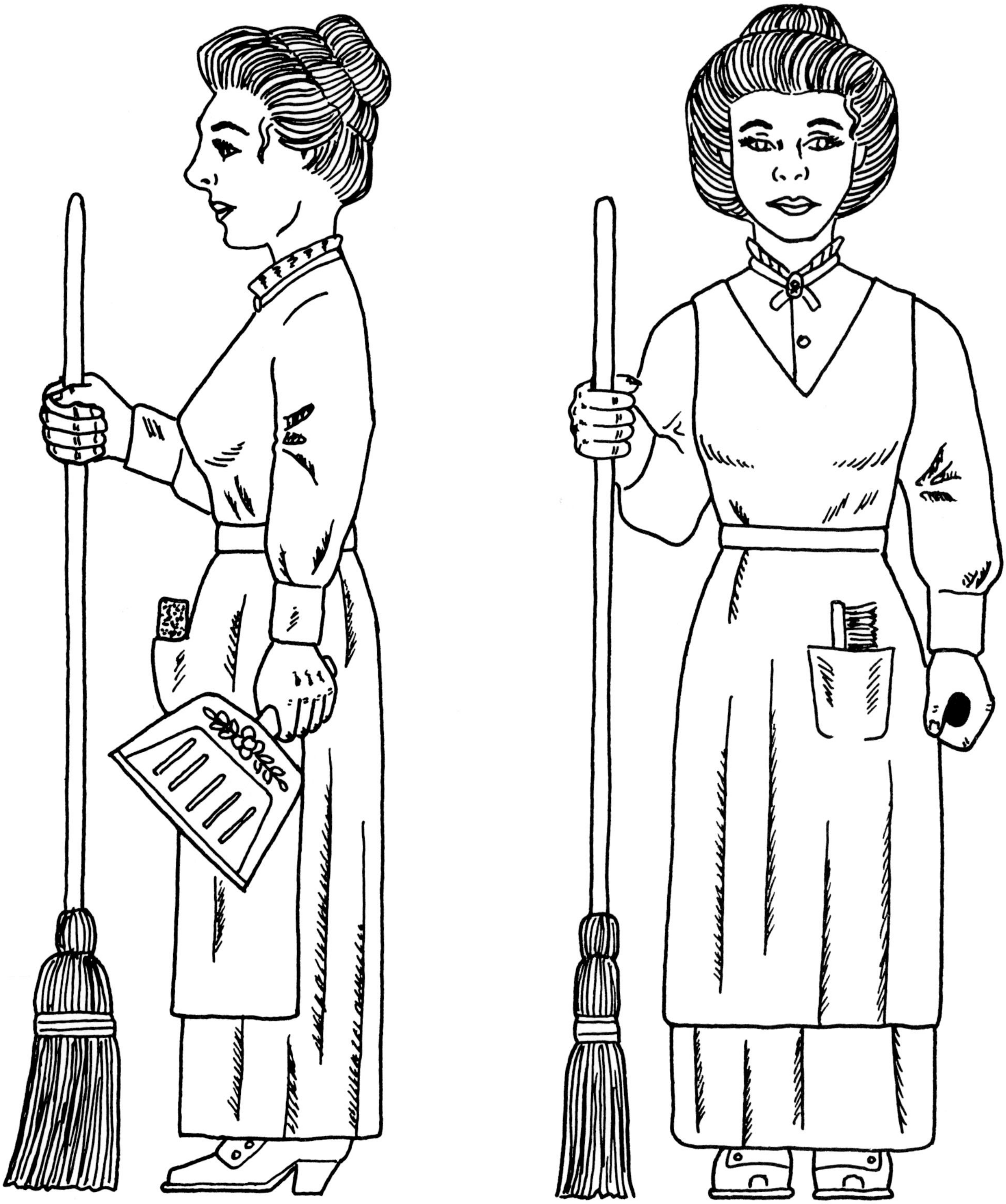

Figure 37 — Pattern for The Housewife

THE EVERYDAY HOUSEWIFE

Again, this is intended to be a book of caricatures, a collection of comic figures blending fantasy and fact as they depict a place and a time.

No one needs reminding of the versatility of women in American history. Names like Carry Nation, Clara Cleghorn Hoffman, and Mrs. William Fordyce mark the pages of Missouri's past.

One of the most outstanding women I have ever known was the lady who ran Parks' General Store in Tightwad, Missouri. Parks' store sold supplies to farmers and travelers for more than seventy-five years, but it was this lady's ice cream and candy counters that are among my fondest memories. She will probably never make the history books. Neither will our "Everyday Housewife". But without them and others like them, there would be no history.

Just as I've chosen to depict the "everyday" cowboy, Indian, and business man over the Bat Mastersons, Cochises, and Carnegies, the "everyday housewife" has "given up the good life" to take her place in this book.

CARVING TIPS

To "liberate" this lady, simply change the hairstyle and clothing. It's the facial features that make women harder to carve than men. But with practice, you should be able to change the pattern and create a number of different female characters.

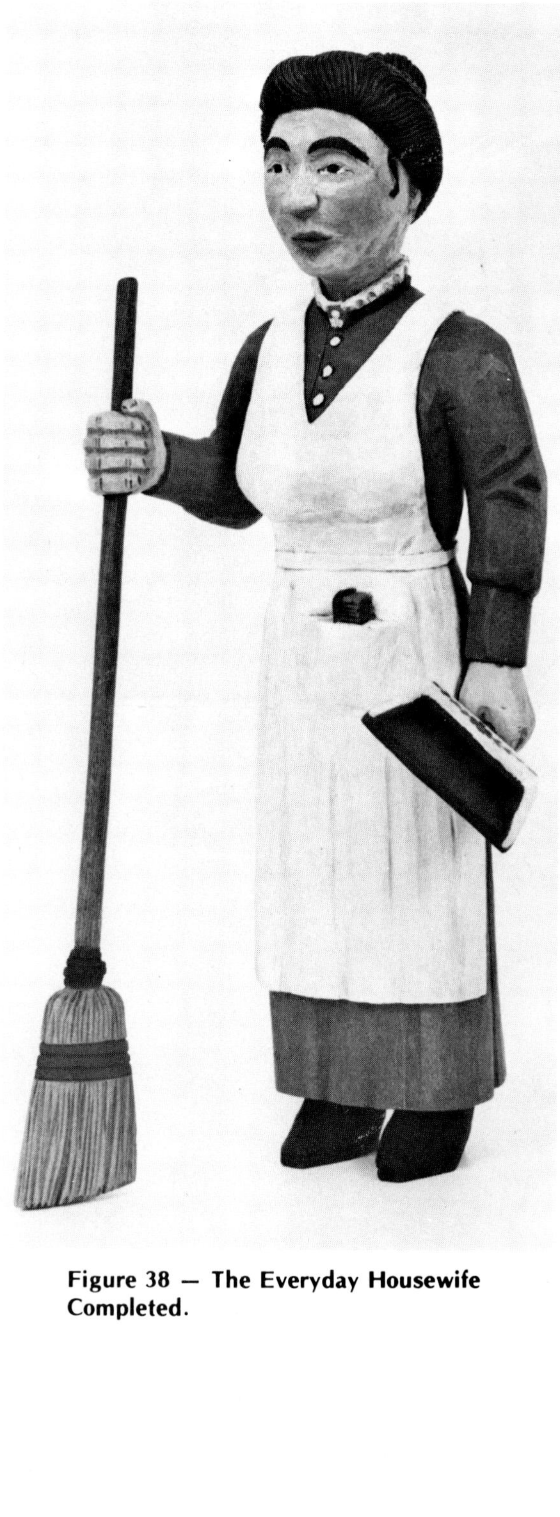

Figure 38 — The Everyday Housewife Completed.

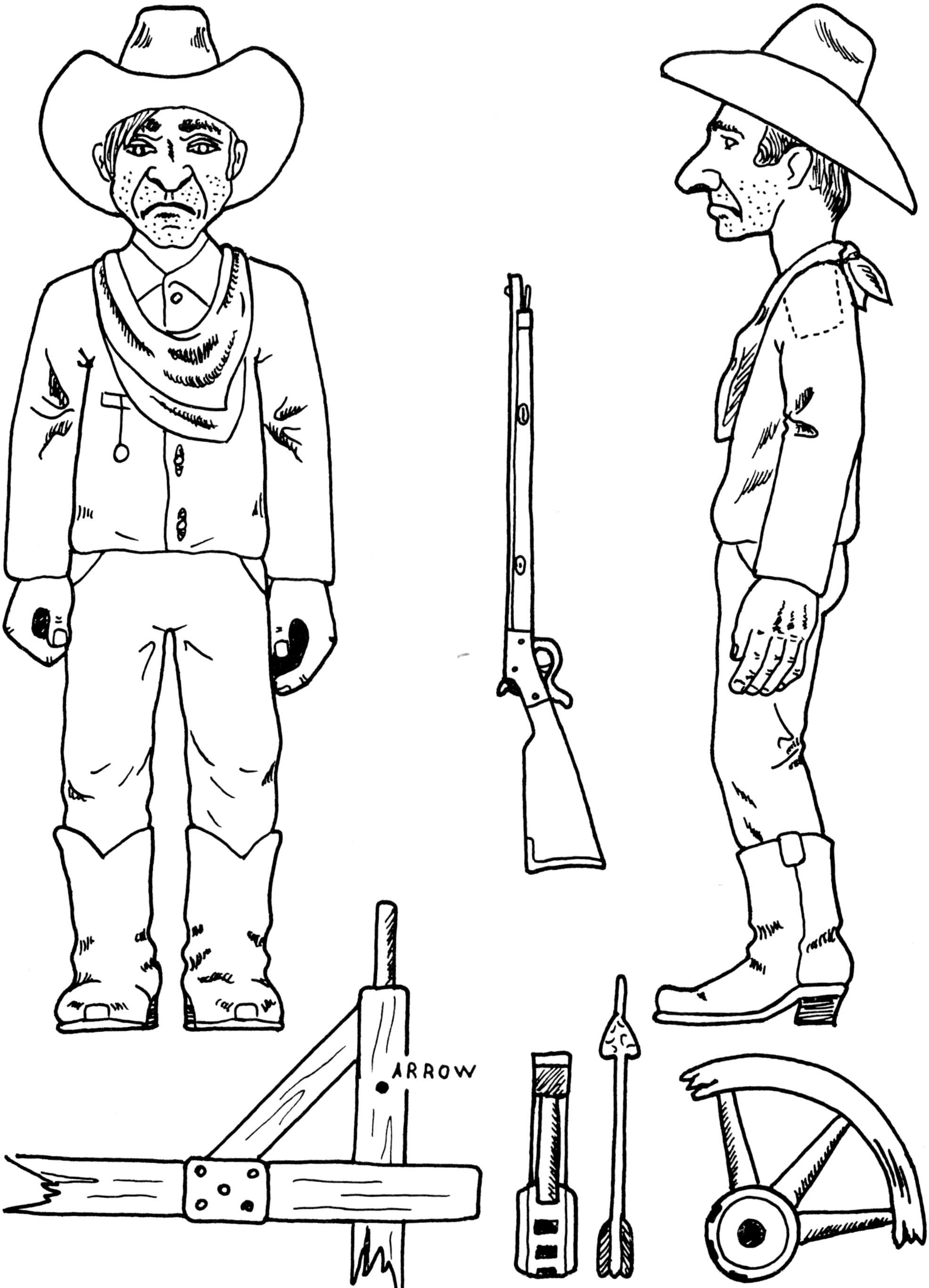

Figure 39 — Pattern for Indian Trouble

INDIAN TROUBLE

Indians have been in Missouri for more than 10,000 years. The treaty of St. Louis, 1818, shows most lands along the Osage River Valley and surrounding hills to be dominated by the Osage Indians.

However, because of its central location and river connections to other regions, Missouri was host to many different Indian cultures. Their villages were scattered along the Osage River Basin until about 1830, when pressure from the U.S. Government pushed them westward.

On occasion, when I want to be alone, I enjoy sitting on the limestone bluffs above the river an imagining activity in the vanishing campsites below. It is an even greater pleasure to walk the freshly plowed river bottom land, hoping to find a flint arrowhead left by those who lived here thousands of years before the whites came.

Were these perfectly chippped stone masterpieces dropped by hunters stalking the giant bison that once roamed this valley? Or are they weapons? Artifacts, surviving time forever, to remind us of false promises, broken treaties, and the price that was paid by our ancestors who settled this land?

CARVING TIPS

Investigating the ruins of a charred wagon, there is little doubt in this intruder's mind concerning the White man's welcome in Osage land.

The wagon is carved in three parts and assembled after carving. You may wish to add more arrows.

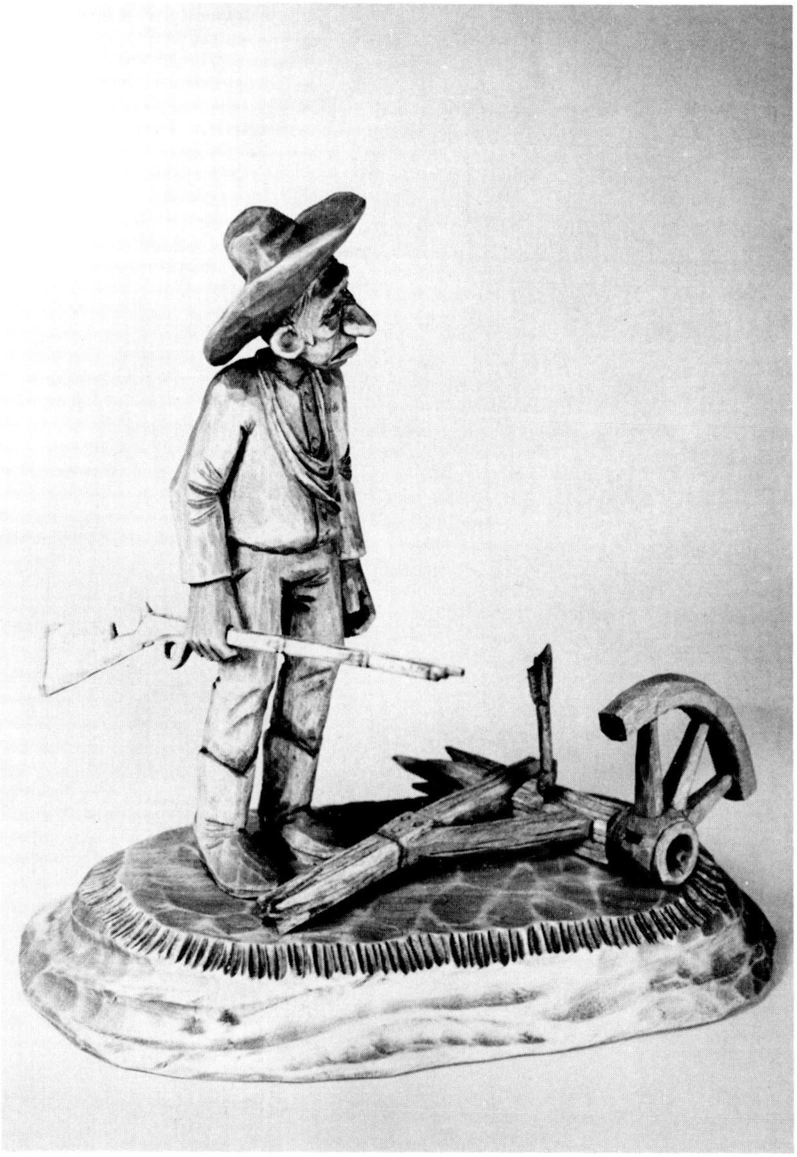

Figure 40 — Indian Trouble Completed.

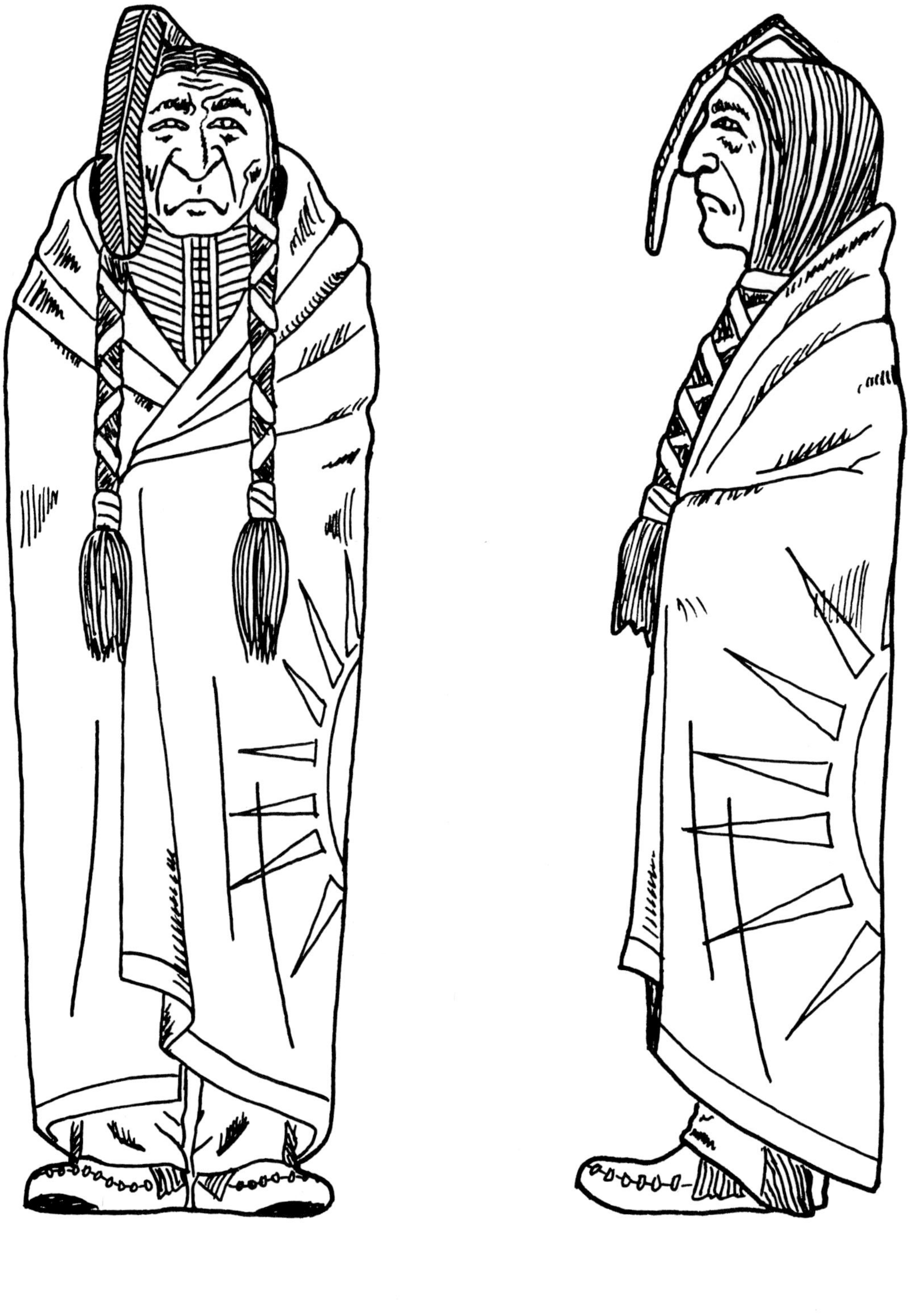

Figure 41 — Pattern for Genuine Indian Blankets and Pottery

GENUINE INDIAN BLANKETS & POTTERY

The American Indian, like the cowboy, is one of my favorite subjects. I enjoy portraying Indians as hunters and warriors, or as the great chiefs of a proud people.

But this is a book of caricatures. And I believe that the creation of a comic or caricature figure should be done in a way that will not offend anyone's culture or heritage.

Too often, the hunter-and-warrior images of American Indian history are emphasized while the artistic aspect is almost ignored. From the charcoal drawings on cave walls thousands of years ago, to the finely woven blankets and beautiful turquoise jewelry of today, Indian craftsmanship is respected and sought after by collectors from all over the world.

It is with this thought in mind that I choose this carving. For, as a fellow craftsman, I, too, have shared the experiences of a slow day at the marketplace.

CARVING TIPS

This Indian is designed to be an interesting figure to carve in and of himself. To make the marketplace scene, add an old box or crate with a few blankets and pieces of pottery.

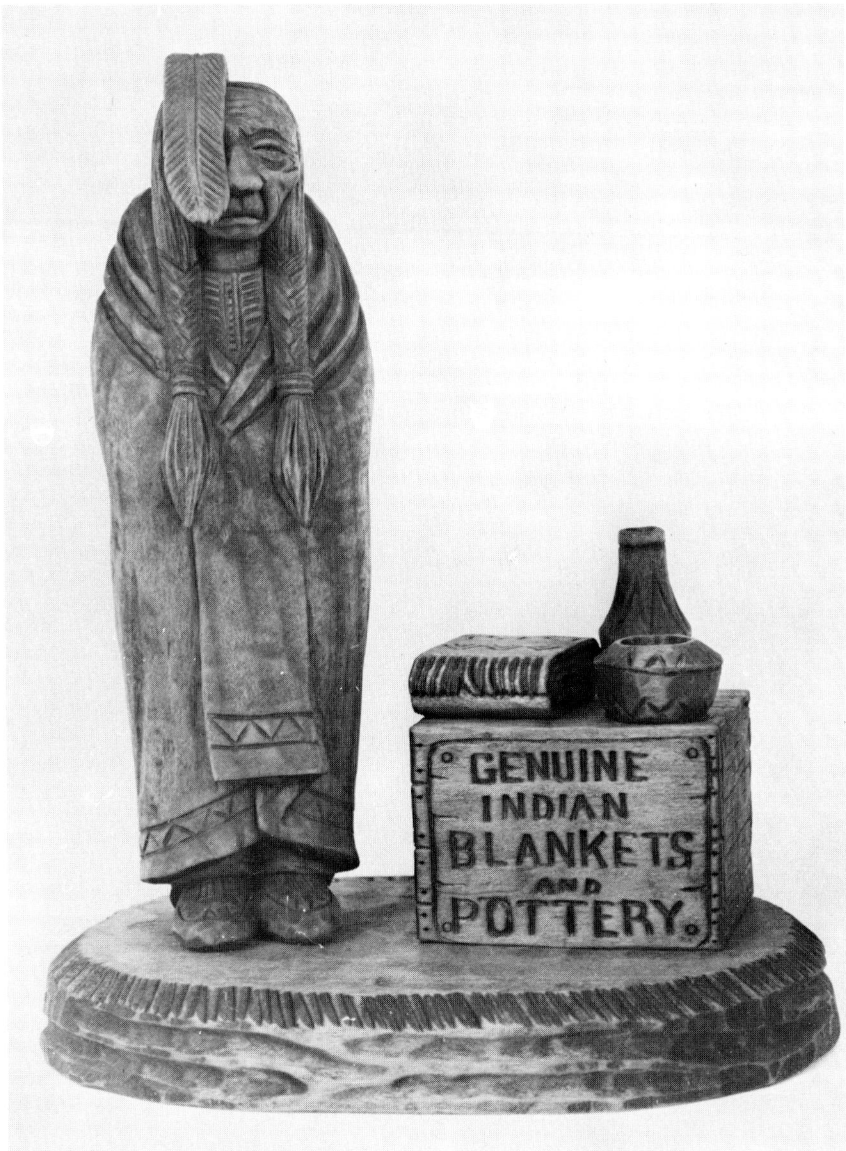

Figure 42 — The Marketplace Scene, Complete With Old Crate, Blankets And Pottery.

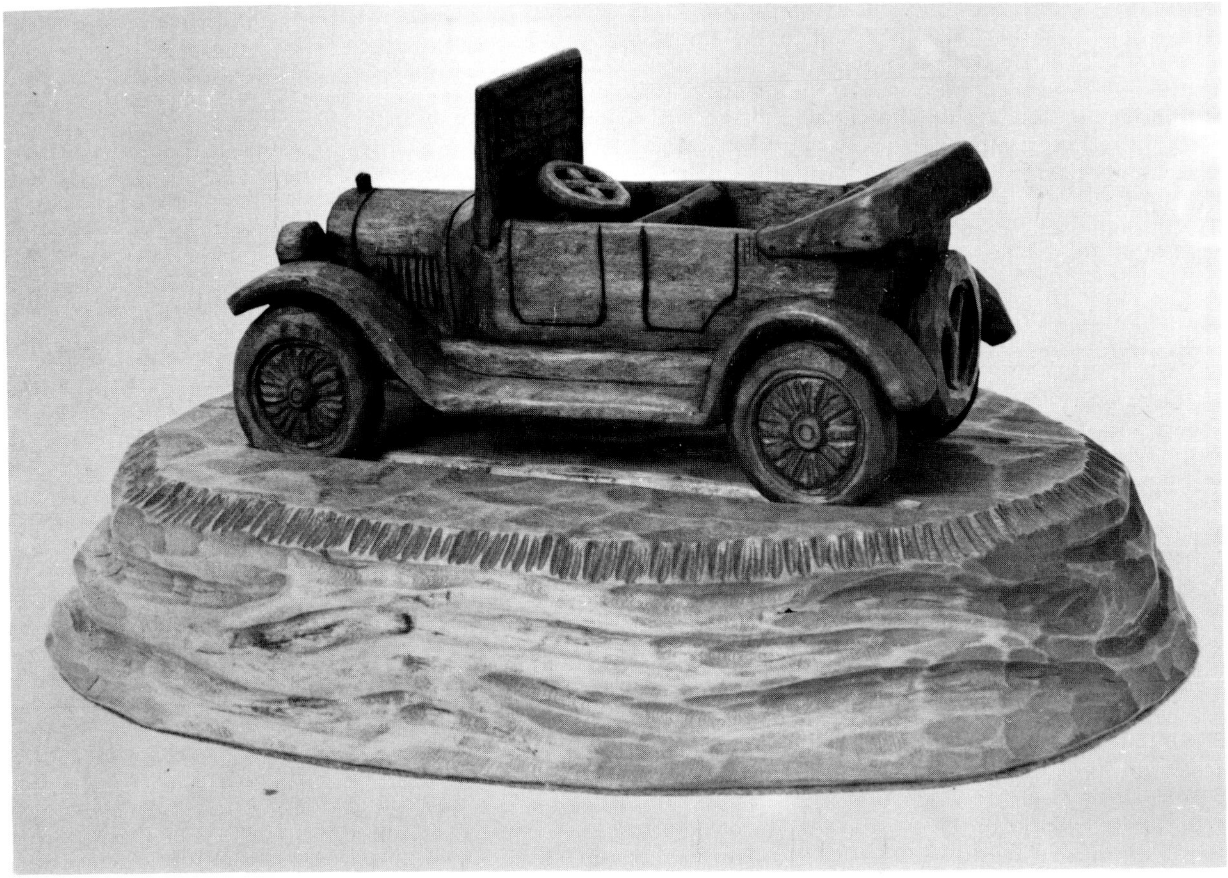

Figure 43 — "Muddy Roads" One of the early day hazards of traveling through the Osage River Basin. Collection of John Lesmeister, Calhoun, Mo.

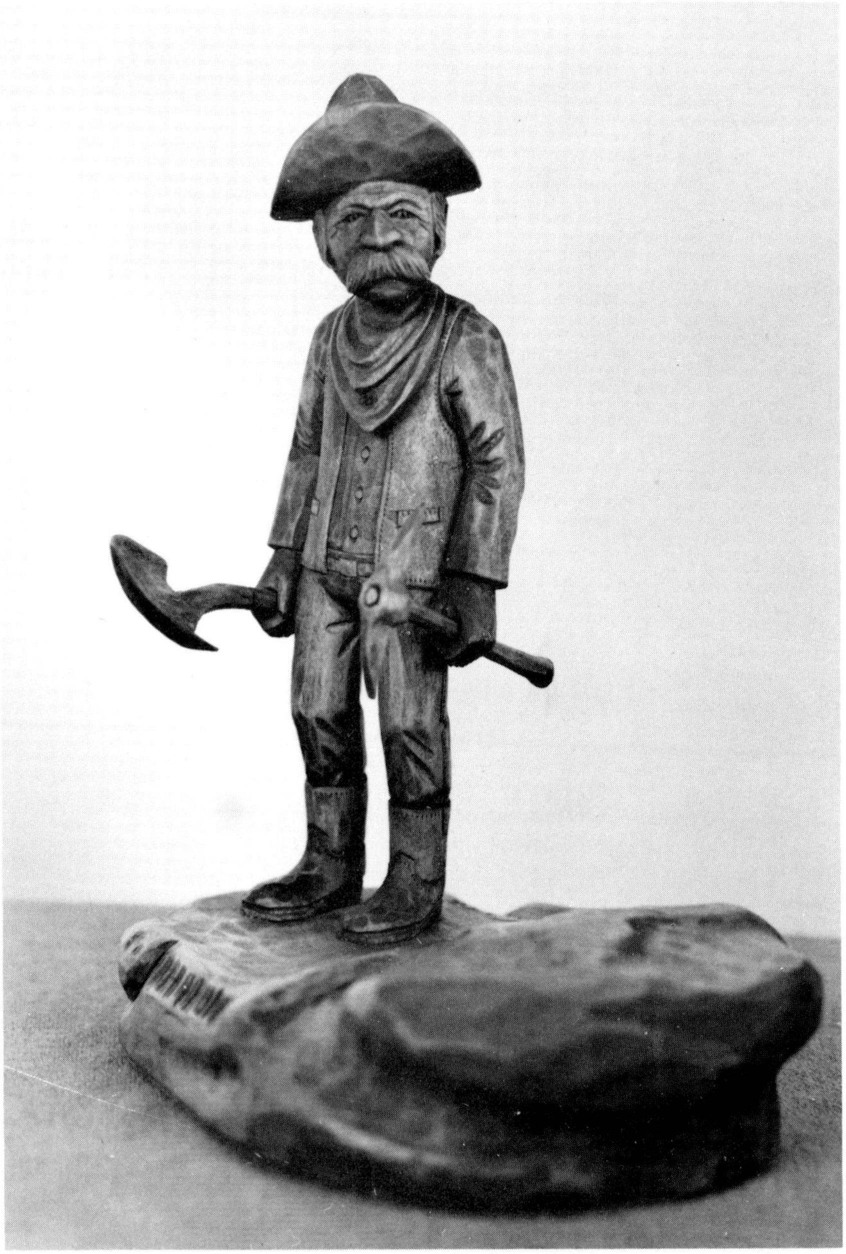

Figure 44 — "Old Prospector" This carving was inspired by a trip to the Colorado gold fields. Collection of Jack Gold, my high school art teacher.

Encyclopedia of Bird Reference Drawings

by David Mohrhardt

"I feel this book will become the one most frequently opened in your studio. You will find it unique in that it offers information not always provided in other reference books". -Bob Guge

This re-issue classic features detailed sketches and wing studies for more than 215 different birds. Includes lots of hard to find information. David is an award winning artist, has been featured at the Leigh Yawkey Woodsom Museum and has a real gift for teaching. We recommend this book as an excellent general reference. Great buy for all carvers, bird lovers and artists.

1-56523-009-4 $14.95

Carving Books by Ivan Whillock

Ivan Whillock is a creative master woodcarver. His books are easy to follow with clear directions and excellent step-by-step photographs and sketches.

Pictorial Relief Carving- projects and patterns
17 projects many photos
Whill2 $9.95

Head Proportions Made Simple
This book will be of real help in understanding what you need to carve faces and figures.
Whill1 $6.00

Carving the Head in Wood- Step-by-step Instruction.
Good clear instructions with over 200 photos cover all aspects from start to finish.
Whill3 $14.95

Carving Characters with Jim Maxwell

New printing of this popular book! Jim has included twelve of his all-time favorite patterns drawn from childhood memories. These projects are designed to be easy to carve whether you are a beginner or advanced carver. These projects feature step-by-step photos and instructions making it easy to quickly understand Jim's techniques and procedures. Want to carve characters? This book takes you from start to finish.

 # Maxwell1 only $6.95

Making Collectible Santas and Christmas Ornaments in Wood.

These 42 easy-to-follow projects will make you very popular this Christmas! Great items for money-making sales as well. This wonderful book presents a variety of projects from traditional to modern, including Santa Clauses and replicas of antique toy ornaments.

Jim and his wife Margie have been making unique carved Santas and wooden Christmas ornaments for over a decade. This new book replaces their earlier book "Carving Christmas Tree Ornaments" and offers eight new, never-before-published patterns for you to make. Highly recommended and a great value.

#Maxwell2 only $6.95

Mammals - An Artistic Approach

Desiree Hajny- to publish first book in Fall 1993.

Nebraska carver Desiree Hajny, well known for her carving seminars and beautiful carved animals will be sharing her knowledge and carving secrets in a new book to be published this fall. Tentatively titled "Mammals: An Artistic Approach" it will be both an excellent reference work on anatomy as well as a complete step-by-step technique book with detailed patterns. This book will start out by teaching you all about mammal anatomy and movement. Then Desiree walks you through some projects step-by-step so you can pick up her tips and techniques in an easy, natural way. Use the patterns to start your own projects then finish it off using Desiree's hair tract burning patterns and painting directions.

Patterns Included: Deer and Fawn, River Otters, Black Bear + more.

Mammals: An Artistic Approach
(Hajny 1) $19.95

WOODCARVER'S WORKBOOK

Best woodcarving pattern book I have seen in my 40 years as a carver!
Ed Gallenstein, President
National Woodcarvers Association

Through her articles in Chip Chats- the National Wood Carvers Association magazine- Master artist Mary Duke Guldan has helped thousands of carvers develop their carving skills.

Follow these complete step-by-step instructions and easy to follow patterns-soon you will be creating beautiful hand carved pieces of your own. A special section on painting and finishing your heirloom carving is found in the back of the book.

Look inside and see for yourself why this book is considered a classic by both beginner and veteran carvers.

This excellent woodcarving manual features patterns for : Cougar, Rabbit, Wolf Dogs, Whitetail Deer, Bighorn Sheep,Wild Mustang Horse,Unicorn, Moose

Woodcarvers Workbook
(guldan) $14.95

Second Woodcarvers Workbook

All-new patterns, projects and techniques from your favorite carving author. This new book will contain more than just animals.

Partial Listing of Pattern Contents
Texas Longhorn, Cows, Bulls and Farm Animals
Native Indian Chief, Elk, Bears

Second Woodcarvers Workbook
Fall 1993 (guldan2) $14.95

Carving Wooden Critters

by Diane Ernst

Curious bunnies, playful puppies- the projects in this book are cute! Delightful patterns at a great price! This inexpensive book features more than a dozen great projects. Easy to follow, clear patterns. Step-by-step beginners' section in front. Great gift and sale items ideas.

(Ernst1) only $6.95